Management's Last Frontier

A Communications System to Focus and Sustain a Culture of Achievement

Ronald George Actis

PEARSON

Custom
Publishing

Printed in the United States of America

10 9 8 7 6 5 4 3 2 1

ISBN 0-536-27327-8

2006160263

EC/SD

Please visit our web site at *www.pearsoncustom.com*

PEARSON CUSTOM PUBLISHING
75 Arlington Street, Suite 300, Boston, MA 02116
A Pearson Education Company

*Dedicated to my parents, Ann and George, and
my sisters Georgianna, Kathryn and Beverly,
whose unconditional love and encouragement gave
me a perfect childhood. And to my wife, Judy, and
children, Greg, Brad, Mark and Cathy, who
perpetuate those qualities and give me
a perfect marriage and family.*

ABOUT THE AUTHOR

Ronald G. Actis is a Management graduate of the University of Illinois. He has 30 years of experience in manufacturing management, labor relations, organizational development, public relations, public affairs, media relations, marketing communications and communications management at General Motors.

He left GM in 1992 as Group Director of Communications and Public Affairs of the former GM Delphi Automotive Components Group and joined Dow Corning Corporation as Director of External Communications.

For the past 12 years, he has been President of Actis Consulting, a change management company.

Actis is an accredited Public Relations Consultant by the Public Relations Society of America and a former adjunct instructor of Management and Business at Saginaw Valley State University.

His accomplishments have been cited in such publications as the *Public Relations Journal, Behavior in Organizations: Understanding and Managing the Human Side of Work* and the U.S. *Congressional Record*. His awards include recognition from the International Association of Business Communicators, the Community Relations Institute, the Chamber of Commerce, the Hispanic Advisory Board and the Black Community Leadership Group along with numerous citations from a variety of civic and charitable organizations.

CONTENTS

FOREWORD

Ron Actis provides a concept of Synchronous Communications Management of special value to corporate communication managers and to students with corporate job placement communication management interest. A former corporate communication manager himself and a current consultant, Actis provides guidance in effectively communicating communication needs to the top management of corporations in a way managers will understand, accept and embrace. To this degree, it may be a revolutionary concept of engaging management support for organizational communication needs.

The father of the synchronous communication concept, Actis defines corporate communication needs and corporate communication strategies using an integrated approach to organizational communication. His objective is to achieve dialogue at all organizational levels by creating and maintaining a culture of shared communication designed to build trust, teamwork, quality performance, and organizational achievement.

What the Actis model does that previous models have not successfully done is that it defines communication as a strategic process designed to achieve specific outcomes in behaviors that is essential for organizational success and stability. To a large degree, the synchronous communication management theory combines communication and change theories, the relationship management theory defined by Ledingham and Brunig (1982), and achieves characteristics of the asymmetrical and symmetrical public relations performance models identified in Grunig and Hunt (1984). Coalition building theory is also inherent in the Actis model because it enables coalitions within organizations to exert increased influence and synergy by working together to achieve effective communication (Tucker and McNerney, 1992).

If the synchronous communications management model had been in place at Enron, the information gap that obviously existed would not have occurred. Enron would not have found itself in a position of finger pointing for communication failures caused by a dysfunctional communication culture. Instead, the culture would have identified problems and needs and a continuous managed dialogue would have assured management responsiveness, if not on the part of top management, then ultimately on the part of trustees and stockholders.

Actis points out to readers that communication failure is directly related to a failure in management and that the failure is due to a lack of recognition of how to manage communication or of the actual cost to the organization of the failure. Enron proved the point.

Actis bluntly admits that most organizational communication is essentially one-way and initiated by the organization's hierarchy. Working within this typical management structure, his strength has been his recognition of how to overcome the communication inadequacies inherent in large organizations.

Basically, he creates a win-win communication and behavioral outcome management style where dialogue is generated through face-to-face communication so that common ground can be found so that understanding and achievement can occur. The Actis approach also achieves management support for the implementation of planned downward in-depth formal communication based on consistency of message, importance to the organization of the communication and timeliness of the delivery.

International practitioners and consultants will also find the concept of special value in working with international clients in bureaucratic, monocratic management structures. Actis provides an organizational communication model with application within many cultures and organizational fields.

Using easy to follow steps combined with examples based on actual experience, Actis uses his communication model as a strategic planning concept to achieve effective communication in complex organizations with multiple levels of employees. His concept provides steps for management, cultural, and communication effectiveness, and for evaluation of a three-way flow of information: to, from and among employees. Basically, he defines a process based on his personal experience within one of the world's top corporations to achieve and sustain a culture of achievement from which all readers of his book will benefit both in knowledge and in understanding of application.

Readers will find his worksheet examples practical, proven, and, most importantly, useable and his Principles of Synchronous Communications Management defined as 10 clear steps they can communicate and apply.

Melvin L. Sharpe, APR, Fellow PRSA
Professor Emeritus Ball State University
1998 Chair PRSA Educators Academy
1998 Recipient PRSA Outstanding Educator Award
1998 Founder, International Public Relations Research Conference
2003 Chair PRSA College of Fellows

PROLOGUE

Setting the stage for integration
of communication and management

Organizational communications is still somewhat in its infancy, perhaps not unlike Frederick Taylor's Scientific Management (SM) concept and Edward Bernays' scientific technique "the engineering of consent" were in the early 1900's. Taylor created the method of breaking-down personnel management into basic subtasks and optimizing performance of the subtasks. Peter F. Drucker brought SM to the ultimate level. Bernays, a nephew of Sigmund Freud, and considered "the father of public relations," combined psychology and sociology with communications to mold public opinion. Communication management still awaits definition.

Although traditional organizational communication is an inconsistent process, most of which is essentially one-way and initiated by the organization's hierarchy, there are some generally accepted effective practices, but, no distinct and specific system. And that is what I have created—a system that incorporates the fundamental elements of communication with the principles of management aimed at achieving specific outcomes.

In today's world, an organizations' leaders pretty well fulfill their function. They plan, organize resources around the plan, direct implementation, and monitor progress to ensure prescribed results. However, they still have difficulty in translating the plan into action and sustaining its focus over time. The problem is ineffective coordination of information sharing—communication management—between leadership and workforce, and among people at all levels in the organization.

The remedy for an organization's information sharing woes is a comprehensive and coherent system, based on applied communication and management technologies, which uses a measured mix of channels, addresses the information needs of management and the workforce and facilitates its flow among them.

It is the missing link I call Synchronous Communications Management (SCM)—a proactive approach to an interactive process of planning, organizing, coordinating, measuring, and monitoring the flow of relevant information downward, upward and laterally which gets the right information to the right audience at the right time by the right channels and creates awareness, understanding, acceptance and actionable support of each issue as a result of continuous follow-through and regular feedback.

A lengthy definition, yes, but one which provides a doctrine that integrates the fundamental elements of communications and management. It completes the mosaic of a strategic, manageable and knowledge-based system to affect information sharing and organizational achievement.

Just about every national communications survey taken of employees during the past ten years finds that the "grapevine" is the dominant source of information within most organizations even though the employees' immediate supervisor and top management are the preferred sources. The majority of employees also says that the organization's communication: is not a priority, has not significantly improved, is not timely, does not tell the full story, does not keep employees sufficiently informed and does not provide for enough upward communications. These surveys do not even take lateral communications into account.

Employees know more about their community and the world around them than about where they work. Why is that? They have few, if any, places to go to find organizational information. On the other hand, they can watch TV and read newspapers and magazines to learn about world current events as they occur.

Outside of the workplace, employees have lives as community leaders and volunteers, vanguards of their churches and synagogues; elected officials of school boards, city councils and county commissions; heads-of-household. They thrive on information. They are enlightened by it—and empowered with it. When they compare the amount of information received outside of the workplace with that available inside, a major gap is conspicuous. And with that, doubt about management's motives and credibility occurs.

Organizational leaders must take heed of these facts and integrate relevant information about operations into the weekly and even daily fabric of the workday. Smart managers will marshal employee inquisitiveness and educate employees about organizational challenges in such a way that employees will understand the challenges and help meet them. To do less is not performing up to their responsibilities as managers.

Sharing relevant information with employees is like giving them the combination to the safe because it shows they are trusted to use the information wisely.

Management in most organization's thinks there is good communication because an internal employee newsletter is published or there is internal e-mail available or an employee meeting is held. But, this is not communication, it is basically informing and much of it is not relevant to the organizations' vision, mission, goals and objectives. In my model of Synchronous Communications Management, informing fits in the "downward" category which is only one-third of an effective process.

With a Bachelor of Science degree in Management and 30 years with General Motors, I gained extensive knowledge and experience about organizational dynamics, management, labor relations, communications, community relations and public relations and was able to put my ideas to improve internal communications into practice and test them.

In recent years as a consultant, I brought the system into a variety of organizations, from corporations and school districts to municipalities and public-service groups, where it was adapted to specific cultures and needs and helped enhance employee achievement. This demonstrated the system's flexibility in small, medium and large organizations with both blue collar and white collar environments.

What I consider to be most important of all is that I have put communications on a scientific and strategic basis and taken it out of the realm of art where its design and production have been fragmented and nebulous. All of the elements have been brought together and put into a communications management system which is issues-driven and aimed at defined outcomes aligned with the organizations strategic direction. And every employee is engaged in sharing information at every level of the organization.

Synchronous Communications Management is not a concept of how internal communications could work. It is a unique, comprehensive, yet simple system, based on successful management and communications practices and experiences, that has proven to heighten organizational accomplishment because it sustains employee focus and actions over time. SCM will accelerate the learning curve in communications improvement and enable rapid enhancement of an organizations' current process and employee performance.

The Synchronous Communications Management system has been noted for its effectiveness in several publications. It was described in a full-length article by the *Public Relations Journal* as "a classic system to share internal information." And it was included as a Case Study "Fixing Communications" in the college textbook *Behavior in Organizations: Understanding and Managing the Human Side of Work* by authors Jerald Greenberg and Robert A. Baron.

General Motors corporate communications head Alvie Smith, now retired, recognized Synchronous Communications as a model for GM worldwide. Smith, Fellow of the International Association of Business Communicators, said: "Saginaw Division has a continuous, diversified employee/management communications system that, without any doubt, is the best in GM worldwide. It's the classic right way to communicate organizational strategy. The key word here is "system" which makes use of all the media and calls for audits of these activities on a regular basis.

"And more than that, this effective system is a process which influences organizational behavior to share information and ideas as a fundamental means of continued progress."

Even more important is Saginaw's demonstrated success in key operational areas. And I know for a fact that employee communications played a central role."

Peter F. Drucker, management guru, in his book *The Essential Drucker*, states that "Communication has proven as elusive as the unicorn."

He said that as all past examples illustrate, the main conclusion of "our experience" with communications is "largely an experience of failure."

Stephen R. Covey, author of *The 7 Habits of Highly Effective People* and *The 8th Habit* and vice chairman of FranklinCovey, says "The most fundamental business issues facing organizations today are focus and execution. There is a serious misalignment between the daily activities of the line worker and the organizational strategy."

Strategy consultants secretly joke about how brilliant their strategies are, based on scientifically derived feasibility studies, but how few organizational cultures execute them. This book *Management's Last Frontier,* strikes at the root of the solution — three-way strategically-oriented communications systems. Ron Actis moved from the top-down, pyramidal control structures and "kiss-up" cultures of the Industrial Age to the empowerment synergistic model Synchronous Communications of the new Knowledge Worker economy. Ron Actis adds tremendous value here, Covey says.

It is my hope that this publication, *Management's Last Frontier: A Communications System to Focus and Sustain a Culture of Achievement,* will be seen as "the definitive workbook" which elucidates the elusive and offers largely an experience of success by helping to align the activities of the line worker with organizational strategy.

It is my intention with this book, to promote executive's, manager's, supervisor's and administrator's awareness and understanding of Synchronous Communications Management as the quintessential tool for managing change and achievement. I urge them to utilize the concept to focus and sustain constructive and productive employee performance. It is also my purpose to encourage adoption of this body of knowledge by institutions of higher learning to perpetuate the technology and offer it in the curriculum to teach students how to better meet organizational needs.

This book is not about what should be done. It is about what has been done and what was accomplished. It is as much for employees as it is for management. It is a comment about how social culture and work culture are intertwined and where disconnects occur. And it is about meeting employees expectations about communications and information sharing at their place of employment.

Some highlights or key content include:

- A review of various articles about communications from newspapers and other publications, and findings from a host of studies and surveys including *Randstad's 2003 Employee Review: Insights into Workforce Communication, Loyalty and Attitudes* and 2004 FranklinCovey research which measures how sharply employees and workgroups focus and execute on their organization's key strategic objectives.
- Significant bottom-line results by use of the system: savings to budget for a seven-year period averaged 3.9 percent at Saginaw Division of General Motors (now part of Delphi Corporation) and totaled millions of dollars; employee suggestion awards went from $864 per eligible employee to $5748 during the same period; employee trust in management and their perception of management's credibility skyrocketed from 44 percent to 85 percent within two years.
- A history of how the system evolved from my ideas and experiences at numerous jobs before graduation from college and at the 30,000-employee Delco Remy and 300,000-employee Fisher Body division's of GM once I had my degree.

- A narration of how all of the elements were brought together into a manageable format at the 30,000-employee Saginaw Division of GM.
- An account of how the sequential 11-point Synchronous Communications Formula and Worksheet were developed while I was at the 300,000-employee GM Automotive Components Group (now Delphi Corporation) and how it can be used as a template to develop communications about any issue in any size organization.
- A four-step management outline of planning, organizing, coordinating/implementing and monitoring the system.
- A listing of the 10 principles of Synchronous Communications Management.

The Addendum presents the other two systems which are part of the Actis Consulting total change management process. These are Applied Management Effectiveness (vision, mission, critical success factors, action strategies and Visible Strategies for tracking progress) and Applied Culture Management (strengthening constructive behavior and eliminating unproductive behavior).

Also, The Addendum includes an Achievement Culture Index that is a composite measurement of Leadership Style Indicators (specific leadership behavioral norms), Employee Perceptions Indicators (employee perceptions of specific management expectations), Employee Empowerment Indicators (employee perceptions of downward and upward communications) and Employee Autonomy Indicators (employee perceptions of lateral communications).

2

WHY THE LAST FRONTIER?

Making the case for a system

The profession of management has come a long way in the past 100 years. From such practice's as "rule of thumb", "intuition", guesstimation", "do as you are told" and "by the seat of your pants", it has advanced to become the strategic driver of organizational success. By today's definition, management plans, organizes, directs and controls every sector of operation. And, by any standard, it has continued to excel in meeting and exceeding the needs and demands of the nation's economy and providing a worldclass livelihood for the populace.

In almost every function of the organization, from engineering to sales and from manufacturing to finance, management has honed them to optimum effectiveness. The exception being communications—information sharing— among its people.

Organizational communications is still somewhat in its infancy, perhaps not unlike Frederick Taylors' Scientific Management concept and Edward Bernays', the father of public relations, scientific technique "the engineering of consent" were in the early 1900's. Taylor created the method of breaking-down personnel management into basic subtasks and optimizing performance of the subtasks. Peter Drucker enhanced it. Bernays, a nephew of Sigmund Freud, combined psychology and sociology with communications to mold public opinion.

Public relations, too, has become much more sophisticated since the days of Edward Bernays, but has not gained in reputation as has management. The term "PR" still conjures up images of flak, snow-job, sand-bagging and bull-shooter.

However, PR is more appreciated in dealing with issues in the public domain than with those inside of an organization.

In virtually every organization that asks its employees to name the area most in need of improvement, the answer comes back "communications." People who work there know more about the world around them and about the community in which they live than they do about where they work. And they are frustrated. And that affects the way they do their job. All because of inadequate knowledge to manage communications effectively.

Various models I have seen that prescribe a process for managing change in human performance suggest that:

- Without a vision, the organization is unfocused.
- Without an action plan, the organization is confused.
- Without resources, the organization is frustrated.
- Without skills, the organization has anxiety.
- Without incentives, the organization is resistant.

Not one of the models of change I have seen identifies communications management as a vital factor. By my definition, communications is the only element of influencing human achievement that can focus on it and perpetuate it. Communication is the glue, the common thread, that can hold the organization together and move it forward.

An article in the *Harvard Business Review* suggests that no organization will change any faster that it can reach the hearts and minds of its people.

I like that statement because it bolsters my ideology about communications—that it provides the only way to reach the hearts, minds and spirits of people and sustain it. It is also the only mechanism that taps into an organizations culture on a regular and consistent basis to get relevant information to its members.

An organizations' culture is another concept that is misunderstood. It became widely recognized as an important characteristic of organizations in the 1980's, but even the experts view culture differently. Two theories emerged. One view is defined by some as the customs, rites, ceremonies, stories, heroes and other patterns within the organization. The other says that assumptions, values, beliefs, behavioral expectations and ideas shared by an organizations' members are what constitute culture.

I think both views make sense. Promoting and maintaining a culture that encourages effective behavior requires using all of the above elements and clearly and consistently communicating them across all organizational levels. Communication provides the message of culture. They are inextricably linked. Effective communication will lead to patterns of behaviors and attitudes that constructively guide the way employees approach their work and interact. Outcomes include trust, attention to quality, teamwork, employee satisfaction and achievement of other goals.

I acknowledge that members of management generally recognize the importance of communications but, they don't know what they do not know about it nor do they know how to truly manage it. And, they don't fully appreciate the power information has on the hearts, minds and spirits of employees.

GOOD EXAMPLES ARE FEW, BAD ONES ARE MANY

In 1996, when Phil Jackson was still coach of the National Basketball Association Chicago Bulls, he and several players were interviewed by *USA Today* about who was the leader of the team success.

At the time, the Bulls had won three league championships and held the best playoff winning percentage in NBA history.

Michael Jordan and Scottie Pippin both said that Jackson was the reason because he "keeps it all together" and is the "ultimate leader."

Jackson meshed the culture of players from four different countries, different personalities and different egos—including Dennis Rodman—into a machine that was 42-5 at the All-Star break.

Jackson said that the secret to the teams success was not prodding. The secret was that they needed to be informed. "They take to information very quickly."

What he did not say was that he was informed, too, and responded accordingly. Thus, sharing information—talking and listening—communicating.

As people who follow sports know, Jackson took his philosophy to the Los Angeles Lakers. He instilled it into each player to the extent that a personality clash of his top stars was transformed into collaborative teamwork and several NBA titles.

Knight-Ridder Newspapers did a story about communications and found that 70 percent of employees think that their organizations communicate no more effectively than they did 10 years ago. And more than half said the grapevine is a major source of information.

The article said that most employees wish to know everything about what is going on. Though organizations generate more data than in the past, they have not been able to harness and disseminate relevant information effectively.

It concluded with a summary of four ways organizations may distinguish themselves for communications effectiveness:

- Effective communicators work hard at letting all employees in on strategic developments such as new products, services, territories, delivery systems, philosophies and structures. Employees want to know where the organization is going.
- Effective communicators are available, open, spontaneous, supportive and transparent. Employees like flesh-and-blood contact with managers.
- There are fewer surprises in organizations where people feel "communicated with." Surprises create distrust and break down commitment.
- The organizations' management sees communication as the essence of leadership.

According to the study, failure to communicate can be costly for companies. Executives said that 14 percent of each 40-hour workweek is wasted because of poor communications between management and staff. That amounts to a staggering seven workweeks of squandered productivity a year.

The American Management Association found that poor communication from upper management is frequently linked to emotionally charged situations at work. Employees said that keeping them "in the dark" affects the way they feel about their organization and hurts morale.

Gantz Wiley Research found that from 1995 through 2001 the percentage of workers who said they "believe in senior management" held steady at about 36 percent.

Their findings indicate that top management builds trust through contact and familiarity. Reaching out to employees through newsletters and meetings helps strengthen that bond. Trust among employees throughout an organization breeds success.

Workers crave honesty more than other qualities of management. Given a list of 28 attributes, honesty was far and above, at 24 percent, the most important to 570 white-collar employees surveyed by Right Management Consultants. Next was integrity/morals/ethics at 16 percent, with caring/compassion a distant third at seven percent.

Experts suggest that managers plan how and what information to share. They agree that without adequate information people live in fear, doubt and confusion. People, they say, don't resist change, they resist the unknown.

A survey by my company, Actis Consulting, of supervisory employees in 40 Michigan organizations found that:

- 67% disagreed that communications are improving there.
- 70% disagreed that they rely less on the grapevine.
- 60% disagreed that they are less surprised by changes.
- 69% disagreed that communication is a priority.
- 65% disagreed that management/supervision listens effectively to them.
- 62% disagreed that it was easier to make their voice heard.

Opinions such as these are not unusual, however, management is unlikely to be aware of them. Conducting communications audits are not commonly done by organizations. Where they are, the questions are not pertinent to the flow of information and the surveys almost never measure responses by job level.

In a recent *USA Today* article, the story compared what coaches and top management did to win trust among their charges. A survey of members of 30 college basketball teams were asked why they trusted their coaches. Players said that: the coach knew what was required to win, he had the players' best interests at heart and he made good on what he said (communications). The study of trust in top management found that employees based their views on integrity, honesty and actions consistent with words (communications).

A story by Newhouse News Service presented a case about gossip filling the information gap in the workplace. It suggested that just as there are dysfunctional families, there are many dysfunctional organizations, places where communications isn't happening the way it should or not at all. And in the absence of trusted, open interactive communications there is a destructive kind of rumor mill.

It goes on to say that gossip and rumor cause the performance of a company to suffer from poor morale and lower productivity. Sometimes it can lead to harassment and lawsuits.

This parallels my thinking regarding the grapevine which exists because of the information gap and is made up of rumor, gossip and half-truths. When employees don't know what is going on, they start guessing and worrying how they will be affected. That causes them to be distracted from the job. Besides, the feeling of insecurity by not knowing is not good for humans.

Sociologists claim that more people are looking for meaning and purpose in life. I think that holds true for work, too.

Perceptions caused by rumors are just as real as perceptions formed from truthful and relevant information. They color what we see, how we interpret, what we believe, and how we behave. How we think about something is reflected in our behavior, so, it is important that relevant information sharing becomes the first among equals in every organization. People yearn for "connectedness" and relevant information helps make that connection and maintains it.

In two-year study a few years ago by the Newton, Mass.-based Center for Workforce Development, researchers conducted "one of the most comprehensive looks yet at learning on the job—the informal education that all workers receive yet few organizations deem important."

According to the report, organizations are searching for ways to better educate their employees and that means pouring millions of dollars into formal training programs. It also means that organizations are ignoring or even frowning upon and discouraging the informal learning that occurs when employees chat with one another at chance meetings, during coffee breaks, during shift changes and during the course of the work day.

During a typical week, more than 70 percent of the 1000 employees who participated in the poll said they share information with co-workers, while 55 percent said they ask co-workers for information.

Further findings showed that most informal learning occurs during meetings, interaction with supervisors, shift changes and peer-to-peer communications.

This study missed the point. It was investigating communications. And it essentially described what I call lateral communications. By managing the flow of relevant information downward, upward <u>and laterally</u>, employees will feel empowered by the information and work more autonomously and collaboratively and learn from one another.

My process would eliminate the need for a huge amount of formal training and substantially reduce the cost of such training. Plus, it would cut the loss of productivity caused by taking people off of their jobs for extended periods of time. Additionally, my system is partially aimed at reinforcing the new skills learned in formal training sessions by expanding that knowledge through formal information sharing across the organization.

Think about it. Training is basically a one shot event. An employees' skill is strengthened, however, rarely is the training repeated on a continuum—annually—to reinforce the behavior. And never is the knowledge shared, by design, with the rest of the organization. So why not accomplish that sharing through the formal communications process.

Although this particular study was billed as one of the most comprehensive yet, its focus was misdirected. This is just another example of how badly communications is misunderstood and why organizational communications is not valued as a powerful, strategic and applied technology. It is also indicative of why communication management's' potential has not been fully explored and exploited.

Newhouse News Service, in an article about information overload, found that electronic communication has overwhelmed the workforce with information. And organizations are allowing it to get worse.

According to a study underwritten by Pitney Bowes, "Managing Corporate Communications in the Information Age," the average Fortune 1000 office employee sends an average of 178 (yes, 178) messages and documents a day. It also indicated that business communications often hinder rather than help productivity of office workers.

Eighty-four percent of respondents said they were interrupted by messages four times an hour, and 71 percent of those questioned said they felt "overwhelmed" by the number of messages they received.

Furthermore, office workers felt they must be attentive to all input because of the office politics involved. One of the messages could be sent by someone who could hamper your career if you fail to read it. And with the number of messages with "cc" attached, the number of people it reaches snowballs to overwhelming proportions.

E-mail was found to be the biggest culprit, however. As one respondent put it: "Check your e-mail, voice mail, fax, Notes database and it's time to go home."

A new take on e-mail comes from Michael Eisner, former Walt Disney Company CEO, who had told graduates at the University of Southern California that the biggest threat to business today is not labor, costs or competition. It is e-mail.

"I have come to believe that if anything will bring about the downfall of a company, or maybe even a country, it is the e-mails that should never have been sent in the first place," he stated, according to The Associated Press.

"I have noticed of late that the intensity of emotions inside our competitive company is higher than usual. I am convinced this is because of e-mail," he said.

"Every fight that goes on seems to start with a misunderstanding over an e-mail."

I have always felt that organizational e-mail is a mixed blessing. The benefits of the immediacy of the message it offers and the capacity for a wide range of distribution are diminished by the number of messages that can bombard employees and interfere with their performance. Organizations should be and are embracing e-mail as a key channel for managed information sharing, but it should not be regarded as the only conduit at the expense of face-to-face contact and printed material. Balancing the media mix is crucial.

NOT A MATTER OF LIFE OR DEATH IN THE TYPICAL ORGANIZATION

During the recent war to disarm Iraq, *USA Today* ran a story, "Information proves vital to strategy," about the Marine Corps' Combat Operations Center and the Lt. General who was responsible for a high number of the land forces confronting Iraq.

Information arrived at the center in floods. Then the information went out to the chain of command to U.S. Central Command in Doha, Qatar and from there to the Pentagon.

"Savvy management of these streams of information is as important to victory in the war as are precision-guided weapons and well-trained troops. The key is: How do you know what's going on? This is a huge organization. We have 85,000 people," said the colonel in charge of operations.

To avoid being overwhelmed by the benefits of too much knowledge, the staff filtered only the highest-priority items, dubbed "commander's critical information requirements," for the Lt. General. Lower priority reports were channeled elsewhere.

At the end of each of the three shifts, status reports of relevant information were exchanged among operations, intelligence and other select departments.

As a student of communications and an observer of its use in a variety of endeavors, this story during the war with Iraq reminds me that continuous coordination of information flow is one of the top criterion for success in any undertaking. Also, the amount of knowledge, skill and time devoted to the process is in direct proportion to the importance of the issue and its outcome.

Just as the stream of information is as important to the military as precision-guided weapons and well-trained troops , so too is continuous information flow as important to organizations as state-of-the-art equipment and well-trained employees.

In war, the outcome is a matter of life or death. In the corporate world, it is profit or loss, survival or liquidation. In schools, it is student achievement or failure.

Whatever the case, information flow should be proactively managed and used as a tool of mass instruction rather than be allowed to incubate as a virus of mass distraction through the grapevine.

In the organizational world, the widespread perception of communications is that it happens—informally—and perhaps through such channels as memo's and bulletin board notices. In other words, management thinks communication takes place if employees are informed about an issue. Maybe the word "communication" itself is part of the problem and confusion because of "uni" suggesting "one way." I prefer thinking of it as "commu<u>union</u>cation" because it suggests a connection between two or more persons who give and take, talk and listen in dialogue.

GREAT MAJORITY OF ORGANIZATIONS DON'T GET IT

Too many organizations, even those that have full-time communications manager's and have some form of process in place, are not addressing enhancements to improve. They seem complacent with what they have. I have come to this conclusion from my consulting business experience. Here are a few representative examples:

- The vice president of human resources and communications for a national retailer said that communication improvements were not needed because they have a state-of-the-art intranet system and they hold store managers responsible for employee communications. The company gets feedback from employees by e-mail. They have no time for formal communications audits because they have to concentrate on the business.

In my opinion, the system is used as essentially downward communications and the manager's have only conventional knowledge of the communications process. The vice president was impressed by the fact that messages could be sent instantaneously and ignored the importance of face-to-face contact and issues communications.

- The director of internal communications for an automotive parts supplier said that it has already "broken the code" for effective communication because it uses employee research from a worldwide consultant and information from an internal employee value study to shape communications. The company saw no need for further improvements in its internal communications process.

The research I have seen pertains to issues surrounding organizational culture and is devoid of implications dealing with relevant information flow about plans, progress and challenges.

- The assistant city manager of a mid-size community said that as a result of the communications assessments I conducted and my recommendations for a comprehensive communications activity, the city decided only to start an employee newsletter on its own.

My problem with doing that is city employees don't understand communications. Their newsletter is nothing more than small talk about who did what in the community, an occasional city business announcement and food recipes.

- After my 30-minute presentation to the superintendent of a medium-size school district—which was "exactly what he was looking for" to address an employee survey that cited communications as the top issue for improvement—a formal proposal to establish an internal communication process, and several follow-up phone conversations, he decided that a web page on the schools' intranet was sufficient.

He was enamored by the medium and impressed that his district was one of the first in the state to install such a system rather than answering employees call for information and dialogue with management.

There appears to be a huge vacuum in the mind-set and attention-span of the above mentioned management and management in general when it comes to communication. They all say it is important, but, seem satisfied with superficial production. Maybe this is due to their: lack of awareness about what it can accomplish; inability to understand how it can be managed; unwillingness to accept that it is a crucial organizational function; oversensitivity for support of the "not invented here" syndrome. Or possibly, the person they have in the position of communications responsibility is the inhibitor.

In March 2003, a study by Towers Perrin in collaboration with the International Association of Business Communicators found that communications professionals are still failing to effectively measure communications despite their interest to address employers' strategic goals.

Informal feedback is used by 57 percent of member organizations, 34 percent use internal interviews and the remainder uses focus group feedback.

Data gathered from more than 1000 electronic survey responses from IABC members worldwide and from in-depth interviews with more than 30 senior communications practitioners confirmed that all are involved in providing organizations with strategic and tactical assistance.

Most respondents focused on helping to improve operating performance and keeping organizations profitable. Improving operating performance is the leading business priority for more than 50 percent of them; 40 percent indicate that "fixing current business problems" is more important than other plans and activities.

While the communications function's priorities included organizational issues and 41 percent said improving the function's productivity is a primary goal, few offered strategies for achieving that end. Forty percent cited support of business objectives, and 36 percent concentrated on strengthening leadership credibility and reducing costs.

Additional findings from the survey: 16 percent listed brand initiatives among immediate communications function goals; 10 percent struggled with the question of how to prioritize activities and task.

"Communication professionals must be able to show the economic return their function generates and how their work contributes to bottom-line business results," said a Towers Perrin researcher. "Since demonstrating economic value is essential in gaining management influence and credibility, communicators must put developing and implementing effective measures at the top of their lists. They can do this through numbers, satisfaction ratings and achievement of particular behaviors."

Most communications professionals have little knowledge of management and the way organizations operate. They probably are journalists or were assigned to communications from the personnel department. Plus they have inadequate skills in organizing and coordinating the process—managing it.

FranklinCovey released the results of its assessment of 11,045 U.S. workers in March 2003. The survey confirmed that most organizations suffer "execution gaps" which undermine the achievement of their highest priorities. The gaps include the following:

44% clearly understand their organizations most important goals.

19% feel a strong commitment to their organizations top priorities.

43% say their organization clearly communicates top goals.

49% say they clearly understand their role in achieving top goals.

40% say their organization's goals are emphasized regularly.

35% say their organization empowers them to meet the goals.

31% say they are provided sufficient direction and feedback.

55% say their organization has a clear mission.

48% say their organization has a clear strategic direction.

37% say they understand the reason for that direction.

14% say workers stay focused on important goals.

38% say managers actively seek employee opinion on improvements.

36% say work team communication is energetic.

52% say they feel safe in expressing opinions.

39% say their work teams communicate freely with other teams.

26% say workers meet at least monthly to review progress on goals.

Overall, workers gave their organizations a score of 51 out of 100 for their collective focus and execution.

FranklinCovey vice chairman Stephen R. Covey gives the following advice to improve focus: "There is no more important activity than for leaders to establish clear, key goals and then communicate those goals to all levels of their organization." The problem is that leaders think they have communicated their goals, but line workers are not aligned with them.

In October of 2003, a major study by Randstad and RoperASW was released. *Randstad's 2003 Employee Review: Insights into Workforce Communication, Loyalty and Attitudes* was conducted between February 20, 2003 and March 21, 2003 based on interviews with 2,826 employees and employers from small-, medium- and large-sized companies and organizations in the United States and Canada.

Overall, the study found a sizable gap in the perception of morale with 58 percent of employees compared with 80 percent of employers saying morale was good or excellent. Morale, the study said, is based on the way people are treated everyday and the resolve and confidence they feel in the vision, direction, and purpose of the company and their jobs.

The desire for a "work family" and to feel in touch and involved with the organization and its leadership is growing. The percentage of employees who said it is important to feel like part of a family was 72 while 82 percent of employers agreed.

"If there is a single theme that weaves through the past four years of research, it is the power of communication. How well you communicate performance expectations, company financial information, provide feedback, and recognize and correct performance has a direct impact on the success of the business," the report stated.

There is compelling evidence that committed employees align their values and goals with the organization's values and goals. To do this they must know and understand the goals, expectations, rewards and consequences.

Workplace communication is improving, but it is an endless process. There is a call for more small and medium-sized meetings and one-on-one conversations when sharing information that is important and critical to the organization. The key to effective communication is focusing on the individual's knowledge, willingness, ability and unique perspective. There is a simple way to make sure your communications is on target—just ask the individual. Employee feedback and two-way communication has to be invited. Employees have to feel it is "okay" to express their thoughts and concerns. They have to feel comfortable approaching management to ask questions and provide their input. Employee feedback must be constantly invited, encouraged and acknowledged. They need to know they will be listened to in a professional, respectful way and that they will be heard.

"If good communication is the most valuable tool for management, then each employee's perception and reaction are the building materials of success. Workplace communication is all about what you are saying and not about how you are saying it," the review said.

Many employers feel they are doing an excellent job of communicating, but so much of management communication is still based on assumptions such as the attitude "If I send it, my employees will immediately understand, agree and do what we want them to do." Employers are sending out more information, but their employees are not getting the messages. Management assumes that communication happens when they press the "send" key. In reality, communication does not exist until the message is received and understood.

More than half of employers rate themselves as excellent communicators. Only 35 percent of their employees agree and 31 percent rate employers as poor or fair.

Nine elements of good communication were used to evaluate performance. The responses of agreement with the statements between employees and employers again showed a substantial difference:

- 74% of employees and 94% of employers agreed that employees were kept as up-to-date as possible about changes at work.
- 74% of employees and 92% of employers agreed that employers gave clear and easy-to-understand information about changes happening at work.
- 73% of employees and 88% of employers agreed that employers did not let rumors about workplace issues get out of control.
- 70% of employees and 93% of employers agreed that employers honestly answered employee's tough questions.
- 68% of employees and 83% of employers agreed that employers gave employees a clear vision of the company's direction and future.
- 67% of employees and 83% of employers agreed that employers communicated even when there was not a problem.
- 60% of employees and 81% of employers agreed that employers clearly explained to employees how changes at work could affect them.
- 42% of employees and 56% of employers agreed that employers told them the whole story and not just give them some information.
- 42% of employees and 53% of employers agreed that employers told employees reasons and factors behind lay-off decisions.

The dark side of this information is that 60 percent of employees feel their employers do not consistently tell the whole story and 50 percent feel employers do not tell the reasons and factors behind lay-off decisions.

What this means is that how well you communicate is more important than ever before. Leaders need to focus on clearly and honestly communicating with employees to keep morale high, employees motivated and loyal to the company.

A commitment to complete, timely, open and accurate communication proves loyalty to employees, and it brings a big payoff for the effort. Employees who rate their employers as excellent communicators have greater faith in top management by more than 2-to-1 over employers who are rated poorly.

The report went on to say that for everyday communication where basic awareness is the objective, 64 percent of employees and 48 percent of employers feel that email and newsletters are effective.

For all their efficiency, email and newsletters are one-way communication. You can send an email message to a vast number of people at one time, but you do not know if the persons at the other end reads and understands the message. Actually, it is the electronic equivalent of carrier pigeon. They assume communication.

In reality, the more critical and important the information the more the need for a meeting for personal interaction, a consistent message and the opportunity to confirm understanding. The message should dictate the channel of communication. Employees (93%) and employers (97%) both say that group meetings and face-to-face meetings are a very or somewhat effective way for employers to communicate about important changes at work.

Employees and employers agree (70%) about communicating early and often. Rather than telling employees about the change after all of the decisions have been made, they feel employers should give partial information as it develops and decisions are made even if things might change in the future.

"For many employers, feedback means telling employees how to do their jobs better. The feedback we have determined as the most valuable is when employees provide input to help the business operate better.

Now, more than ever, you should do more. Don't just talk—ask for input and take action ... even if nothing changes. If positive results come of it, there's a big bonus. Just asking doesn't make employees feel valued. Acting on what they tell you is a major influence on loyalty."

Among employers who ask for feedback, 97 percent of employers claim to take action, but only 86 percent of employees say they do.

Three-fourths (77%) of employees who say their employers ask for feedback and take action, feel important and valued while only 39 percent who are not asked feel the same.

Feedback has a similar association with more faith in top management. There is a 43 point gap between asking for feedback but not taking action (52% have faith in top management) and asking for feedback and taking action that results in positive change (95% have faith in top management). What is clear from this information is, if you have an issue and you are not prepared to take action, it is better not to ask.

Nine out of ten (91%) employers say they want to hear employees ideas, opinions and suggestions, yet only 69 percent of their workforce believe them. Thirty percent of employees think their managers just want them to blindly repeat the company line.

"Every organization has its official communications channels. And then there is the "Grapevine" ... the invisible network that spreads information, rumors and gossip."

The Grapevine is far more powerful than management realizes. More than 8 out of 10 (83%) employers think that they are the first to tell their employees about changes or decisions at work. Only about half of their employees agree: 46 percent hear it first through the Grapevine.

At its best the Grapevine reflects the health of an organization by showing what is on people's minds. It builds relationships and a feeling of belonging. At its worst, it breeds paranoia, discontent and bad morale. Nearly three-fourths (72%) of employees agree that the Grapevine is more likely to spread negative information than positive.

Negativity can infect the entire organization. Employees with negative attitudes expect the worst to happen. They tend to complain a lot and resist change and new ideas. They are not motivated and can cause an unproductive environment.

Since employees are more concerned about being part of a "work family," then talking and sharing information is human nature. When faced with change, the Grapevine helps to satisfy the employees' need for knowledge and security. The sense of being inside a group, the concept of safety in numbers, helps to make everyone feel more secure. In the absence of reliable information and when people do not know what is going on, they will fill the vacuum with the worst possible scenarios. They will just make things up. If the only information on the Grapevine is malicious gossip, then people tend to believe the gossip. The more they worry, the more they turn to the Grapevine and the less productive they become. Almost 50 percent of employees first hear about major news and rumors on this informal channel.

Almost half of employees and more than half of employers agree that information from coworkers about things going on at work turns out to be wrong. Most (83%) of employees say they are comfortable going to a supervisor to confirm the accuracy of information on the Grapevine. And, 87 percent of employers think their workforce has no reservations about verifying rumors.

Encouraging employees to go to management with questions and coaching management on how to properly handle these concerns, could help stop the spread of inaccurate, incomplete or inadequate information.

In its conclusion, the report states "How well people at the top are instilling a sense of ownership, confidence, stability, inclusion and direction in the workforce makes the difference. Companies that are actively developing ways to inform, inspire and reassure their employees are being rewarded with higher loyalty, morale and employee confidence. Communication is the key.

Management has been making strides to improve how they communicate, but as good as it may be now, it needs continuous improvement."

This is an outstanding study. But the question still remains How to do it?

I became aware of this study from USA Today. *Two small charts were published on consecutive days to illustrate employee and management perceptions about communications. I called Randstad to obtain more information and was sent a copy of the report. I was impressed with its scope and thrilled that many of its findings and conclusions were so close to my beliefs and expectations.*

The review confirmed what I had been thinking and preaching for a long time—the gap between management's perceptions of communications and employee perceptions is a wide and significant one. And it highlights the fact that an organizations leadership has not come to grips with the many nuances of communications management.

The other question that lingers in my mind is How many other people know about this study? USA Today *only shared two charts.*

In a December 2004 interview by the Boston Globe's Robert Weisman, Stephen Covey says that his new book, *The 8th Habit*, identifies the habit of finding one's voice and inspiring others to find theirs.

"There is a deep, innate, almost inexpressible yearning within each one of us to find our voice in life. The exponential, revolutionary explosion of the Internet is one of the most powerful modern manifestations of this truth," Covey writes.

In the organizational world, this new reality opens the possibility of fulfillment and significant contributions from employees, however, many of them remain alienated Covey argues. The majority of workers don't trust their employers, are unenthusiastic about corporate goals and lack a clear understanding of what their organizations is trying to achieve.

"The fundamental problem is we are using an Industrial Age paradigm in a knowledge-based economy," Covey said. Some companies are learning to take advantage of communications and tap into the wisdom of employees. But others, including much of the U.S. auto industry, have shown a reluctance to abandon their traditional ways and forge partnerships with employees.

I could not agree more as illustrated by the following.

An August 1997 *Detroit Free Press* interview, with David Cole, director of the Office for the Study of Automotive Transportation and now at the Center for Automotive Research, about vanishing boundaries in the auto industry revealed that he thinks the auto industry as a whole has a culture that is more "malleable and flexible" than the Japanese or Germans.

"We may have a better ability to make the cultural changes that are associated with the world that is emerging," Cole said.

The Japanese and Germans are very good at product development and some other areas, he said. But can they go to the next level?

That next level is agile manufacturing linked directly to product development and marketing—a seamless organization—where the gain is competitive advantage.

When asked if he thought Detroit carmakers were ready for a change of that magnitude he said, "Intellectually, the leadership has a pretty good understanding of what they want to do. On the other hand, I think when you start looking at it in terms of the actual troops who have to make the transition down inside the organization, it's tough."

As a result of that article, I wrote to David Cole and asked to talk with him about my communications system. He was fascinated with what I had developed and with what I had accomplished with it. He agreed that such a system was much needed to help management deal with the "soft-side" of the organization—the people. We discussed possible pilot programs in the auto industry to more fully demonstrate its effectiveness to management, but were not able to obtain sponsorship. There was no interest in communications.

Most of the preceding discourse has to do with information. However, a succinct example of what is absent, yet key to achievement, follows in other stories from the world of sports.

The first sentence in the *Detroit Free Press* article "Nets hang on Frank's every word" asks the question: "What's the secret to Lawrence Frank's success?"

Frank, the 33-year-old former assistant coach of the NBA New Jersey Nets who was named head coach just before the league's 2004 All Star Game, broke the 10-0 NBA record with a 13-0 start to an NBA coaching career. He also erased the 12-0 modern North American mark for the best coaching start in professional sports.

He is known to be a good communicator and gives inspirational pregame speeches. His players say that Frank's tells them not to get distracted.

"He tells us "Don't get distracted by what we did last week or by the next opponent or by what's going to happen next week. Focus on one thing at a time," says Nets center Jason Collins.

Focus is the key word here. All the relevant information in the world will do no good if it is not focused. Clearly, it is easier to coach a basketball team of a dozen players or so than manage an organization of hundreds or thousands of employees. But, through intelligent coordination of information topics and flow, communication managers can minimize distractions and focus the entire workforce on what matters most to organizational success.

Frank's job has just begun. He got started on the right track by focusing his players. Now the task is to sustain that focus. Whether a sports team or an organization, the challenge is the same.

Joe Torre, New York Yankees manager, does essentially the same as Frank and added a twist about autonomy in a *USA Today* article. He said that he brings the team to Spring training focused on just one thing—winning.

"Baseball is a team sport, but it's more of an autonomous sport. Nobody has to work in concert except the second baseman and shortstop (for double-plays).

"I'm the manager and my feeling is that if we're thinking about winning as opposed to how far I can hit the ball or how many guys can I strike out, we're going to approach the game differently."

Comparing communications in sports with that in organizations may sound like comparing apples and oranges. But, a closer look reveals that when it comes to the human condition, the similarities are huge. People are people are people. They have dignity and want respect and validation of who they are.

Some may rationalize from the above illustrations that although a large minority of employees is not being reached by the organization, a majority is receiving information. Why isn't that number 100 percent? This may be yet another indictment about management's lack of awareness of communications' influence on employee behavior and the question of communication executive's acumen and leadership abilities.

Peter F. Drucker, in his book *The Essential Drucker*, states that "Communications in management has become the central concern to students and practitioners in all institutions. In no other area have intelligent men and women worked harder or with greater dedication than psychologists, human relations experts and managers."

"Yet communication has proven as elusive as the unicorn."

He adds: the main conclusion to management's experience with communications is largely an experience of failure. Communications is not a means of organization. It is the mode of organization.

I could not have said it better.

Consequences to ineffective communications in the great majority of organizations are not a matter of life and death. Profit or quality or customer satisfaction or people's feelings may be affected, but usually nothing happens that cannot be corrected or amended. Tragically, consequences were that severe in the disaster of NASA's space shuttle Columbia.

The Columbia Accident Investigation Board released its report on August 26, 2003. It said "The accident was probably not an anomalous, random event but rather likely rooted to some degree in NASA's history and the human space flight program's culture."

The report listed the contributing factors: "reliance on past success as a substitute for sound engineering; organizational barriers that prevented effective communication of critical safety information and stifled professional differences of opinion."

It appears that lack of communications is faulted as one of the key conditions leading up to the terrorists attack in the United States on September 11, 2001.

During testimony to the 9-11 Commission, Condelezza Rice, former National Security Advisor, summed up what many suggested—there were structural problems—information was not shared.

Former Attorney General Janet Reno said " The FBI didn't know what it had. The right hand didn't know what the left hand was doing."

Why the last frontier? I rest my case.

3

BOTTOM LINE RESULTS

Creating dialogue improves productivity and profitability

Just as an organization may track profit or attainment of goals and just as a sports team notes statistics on every key ingredient to peak performance, so too must indicators of communication effectiveness be determined and recorded.

Managers must learn to calculate the impact of their words and actions as precisely as they compute the bottom line. Communication without purpose and results is opportunity lost. They must walk the talk and measure that correlation because actions certainly speak louder than words.

It's said "That which is measured gets done," (and institutionalized). In that vein, I'll begin with some results obtained by use of the Synchronous Communications Management (SCM) system to illustrate the power of the concept as a strategic management tool. It helps shape an achievement-oriented and productive organizational culture which constructively impacts management and employee behavior and the bottom line, with nominal investment. A "few" knowledgeable and skilled communication managers are able to mobilize the efforts of thousands and move them into action to achieve organizational goals and objectives.

The SCM system requires planning, organizing, coordinating, measuring, and monitoring the flow of relevant information downward, upward, and laterally throughout the organization on a daily basis.

Synchronous Communications provides an issues-driven format which facilitates strategic thinking and decisions regarding getting the right information to the right audience at the right time through the right channels to create awareness, understanding, acceptance and actionable support of goals and objectives.

GENERAL MOTORS, MY MAJOR TESTING GROUND FOR SCM

When I was public affairs director of GM's Saginaw Division, the system gained recognition as the best communications process in General Motors, worldwide, and was considered a model for the corporation. Alvie Smith, former GM Director of Corporate Communications and Fellow of the International Association of Business Communicators, said "Saginaw Division has a continuous, diversified employee/management communications system that, without any doubt, is the best in GM worldwide. It's the classic right way to communicate organizational strategy. The key word here is "system" which makes use of all the media and calls for audits of these activities on a regular basis.

"And more than that, this effective system is a process which influences organizational behavior to share information and ideas as a fundamental means of continued progress."

Even more important is Saginaw's demonstrated success in key operational areas. And I know for a fact that employee communications played a central role."

The system also received attention from international communicators and has been featured in various journals, magazines and books, including college textbooks as a case study.

Roger D'Aprix, consultant with William M. Mercer at the time, told a seminar at the International Association of Business Communicators in London that GM's program was the most methodical assault on the problem of internal communications he had ever seen. He had already observed and examined the Saginaw system.

The Synchronous Communications Management system has been noted for its effectiveness in several publications, described by the *Public Relations Journal* as "a classic system to share internal information" and included as a case study in the college textbook *Behavior in Organizations: Understanding and Managing the Human Side of Work* by authors Jerald Greenberg and Robert A. Baron.

For communications to bring value to the organization, it must significantly and positively impact the bottom line and other key organizational indicators of success. Much of the information disseminated today is superficial. It does not pertain to organizational vision, mission, plans, issues, challenges, and the like. And the same information is essentially given to everyone rather than targeted to specific internal audiences.

During my seven years at the former 30,000-employee Saginaw Division of GM, now part of Delphi Corporation, I was able to put my communication ideas and theories into practice. The focus was Saginaw's strategic business plan.

Several critical areas of performance were targeted for improvement and achieved. Among them were:

- Year-to-year budget savings went from 2.8 percent the first year, up to 4.9 percent the second year, then to 3.2, 3.7 and 2.2, then soaring to 5 and 5.5 percent which, at GM, amounts to millions of dollars not spent.
- Aftermarket/ replacement parts delivery on time went from 60 percent to 100 percent on time in a matter of months.
- Sales per salaried employee doubled.
- Savings from suggestions for one year went from an average of $864 per eligible employee in 1981, to $1,220, $1,306, $1,743, $1,547, then up to $2,305, and more than doubling to $5,748 in 1987. The $5,748 amount placed Saginaw Division first among GM's 24 reporting units. Although its workforce accounted for only 3.7 percent of the eligible employees for GM's Suggestion Program, it produced 16.1 percent of the corporation's Suggestion Program savings.
- Employee trust in management and their perception of management's credibility skyrocketed from 44 percent to 85 percent in the first few years.
- The divisions' Internal Customer Satisfaction Index increased an average of 20 percent per year.

Other members of the Saginaw Division executive staff agreed that although many employees efforts went into such impressive accomplishments, Synchronous Communications Management was the enabler that made it happen. It was the key that opened dialogue between management and the workforce and among employees at every level. This was a monumental shift in the leadership's perception of what communications management can do.

Another notable benefit derived was the improved relationship with the unions at four Saginaw Division locations in the United States. Union leaders said that it was the first time cost figures were shared with them and the first time they understood some of the major issues and challenges of the division were truly competitive ones. They said, too, that it was also the first time the union had a voice in the communications process. Clearly, this had a positive sway on future labor relations and contract negotiations.

There also was a spin-off gain made in the Saginaw, Michigan community because of the new alliance with union leaders. Saginaw Division general manager W. Blair Thompson, who later was named GM group vice president in charge of what became Delphi Corporation, and I formed the Business-Union-Government (BUG) Group for Economic Development to assist the area in business and job retention and attraction.

Members of the steering committee included the Saginaw Division United Auto Worker Local 699 president and bargaining chairman. This encouraged other union leaders from 40 area locals to participate in the groups monthly meetings and activities with their management counterparts. Other members of the steering committee included the incumbent congressman and state legislator, county commission chairman, and city manager.

To draw state-wide attention towards this collaborative body and reinforce the fact that Saginaw Division needed the support of its employees and unions as well as support of local, state and federal governments, the new general manager, Mark McCabe and I proposed that an economic summit be conducted by the BUG Group.

More than 200 area business, union and government leaders attended the summit at the Saginaw Civic Center to hear comments from GM vice president of Industrial Relations Al Warren, UAW vice president, GM department, Don Ephlin, The University of Michigan's director of management projects for the Office for the Study of Automotive Transportation, Larry Harbeck, UAW Research Department economist, Bruce DeCastro, U.S. congressman, Bob Traxler and others including Mark McCabe.

Warren said that the success of the joint process—union leaders and employees working with management—is essential for the continued success of General Motors. He said there is no doubt that employees know more about the job than any member of management does or will ever know, so employees must be enrolled in the battle if GM is to be more competitive.

Ephlin pointed to the "good old days" when GM internal suppliers had it made because they had ready-made customers and did not have many demands on them. He said it was different now because of competition and that every GM unit must be looked at as an independent business. Achieving that edge will require everyone's input.

Harbeck stated that the auto industry led the world in productivity, but fell behind the competition particularly in the employees per vehicle ratio. Success in the industry will ultimately depend on cost reduction and quality improvement.

DeCastro offered the question of "What will happen if GM and the unions chose not to accept the realities of the marketplace?" He said that at GM's current level of vertical integration (before Delphi was spun-off by GM) each point of marketshare lost was worth about 7,000 jobs.

Traxler pledged to work more closely with the industry and repeated his support for emission controls that were cost-benefit oriented.

McCabe closed the conference with a statistical eye-opener. He said that 66 percent of Saginaw's products were competitive in the world marketplace, while 34 percent, to which 3000 jobs were associated, were in a threatened position due to higher cost factors. He called for all segments of business, unions and government to pull their resources together to help Saginaw.

The summit was widely covered by the Michigan media which gave credence to the information communicated inside the division. And, over the course of the following 12 months, what was said by the speakers was reported in the division's daily newsletter, monthly tabloid and bi-monthly video program. Employees, particularly union members, sat up and took notice of what their leaders had to say about competitive issues. They also took productivity improvements and cost reduction more seriously.

Because of the BUG Group, there is an economic development agency, Saginaw Future, in place today which brings together the county, city, townships, chamber of commerce, business, unions, education and government to pool resources in a unified effort to help business create jobs. Saginaw Future was named one of two top agencies in Michigan for development projects at that time.

SCM HELPED RESOLVE OTHER PROBLEMS TOO

I used elements of the early SCM system and resolved a 13 year-old environmental problem when I was at GM's former Fisher Body Division in Lansing, Michigan. This was a true PR nightmare. It generated a huge amount of negative publicity and irritated civic officials and residents of a large neighborhood adjacent to the plant.

The *Lansing State Journal* published an editorial commending Fisher Body for fixing the problem and cited its outstanding corporate citizenship. A major fringe benefit came from the city council approval of a $50 million tax abatement for new Fisher Body plant equipment and facilities which would not have happened without elimination of the air pollution.

In recent years as president of Actis Consulting, a change management and communications company, a major challenge was resolved by use of the Synchronous Communications Management system involving the nutrition and food service department of one of the largest school districts in the nation. The district has more than 200 elementary and secondary schools and a budget of $1 billion. Food service has 2000 employees serving 160,000 meals a day, including breakfast, and cafeteria food sales of $65 million annually.

Actis Consulting was retained to assist the Executive Director of Food Service to improve staff collaboration and performance. There was confusion among managers and the staff about their role and the strategic direction of the department, low morale, and little interface and trust between management and staff. Diversity was also an issue according to the staff. The executive director was white while Hispanics and African Americans made up the majority of the staff.

Communications management was chosen as the catalyst for improvement with support from two other Actis systems—Applied Management Effectiveness (AME), which defines strategic direction, and Applied Culture Management (ACM), which promotes specific constructive management and employee behavior.

Employee ratings of communications increased in several key areas, among them:

- Overall, employees are kept well informed—from 61% to 91%.
- I know goals and objectives of the organization—from 60% to 95%.
- I know and understand the vision and mission—from 72% to 100%.
- Changes are well communicated to employees—from 65% to 92%.
- My immediate supervisor listens to my ideas, suggestions—from 81% to 91%.
- I speak about work with employees in my department—from 75% to 100%.

The department was recognized by the state comptroller's office for exemplary performance in reducing food costs 13 percent and labor costs six percent, significantly increasing employee retention, improvement of accounting and reporting procedures and overall cost effectiveness. The district superintendent cited the department for superb management practices in achieving its strategic plan and conformance to all state and federal nutritional and sanitary standards. It was named a model operation for school districts nationwide.

In addition, the executive director received the Silver Plate Award from the worldwide 680-member International Foodservice Manufacturers Association as the outstanding leader of the year for elementary and secondary schools for creating a model organization.

Application of the SCM system in a municipal township of 75,000 residents and its staff of 200 employees not only resulted in giving taxpayers more and better services for their tax dollars, it boosted the effectiveness of the department heads and township manager which resulted in a near-perfect township trustees appraisal of the managers' leadership performance.

Adoption of SCM and the Actis Applied Management Effectiveness (AME) system by an urban elementary school in a medium-size city strengthened the leadership skills of the principal, increased the focus and collaboration of school staff and helped improve student reading scores to one of the best in the district. AME was designed to help the organization to more clearly define its vision, mission and critical areas, then track the action strategies to successful completion. AME also provided the focus for the Synchronous Communications system. In other words, what an organization plans to do, it also plans what to communicate.

Another example of SCM's strong influence and results took place at a high school in a major city. I was called by one of the area superintendent's of that school district to counsel her and the school principal in establishing a stronger bond between the principal and staff and the principal and students. The call to me was triggered by a student walk-out of classes a few weeks earlier.

After interviews with the principal, teachers, students and even parents, I conducted our Communications Effectiveness Inventory and Culture Inventory to determine the strengths and weakness of communications and the behavioral norms and values of the culture. As expected the weaknesses were many and the culture was not conducive to our motto of collaborate, create, achieve. The biggest inhibitor was found to be the principal.

I developed a communications plan which called for, among other things, a school newsletter for the staff, a newsletter for the students, a calendar of mandatory meetings for the staff, and a revival of the Parent-Teacher-Association. The plan also included a Communications Philosophy Statement which described the communications role of the principal, teachers and students, and contained specific activities for parental involvement.

One year later, problems at the school were almost non-existent and the naming of a new principal the following summer further enhanced the culture there.

When I used the SCM and AME systems as chairman of the Saginaw County, Michigan, Chamber of Commerce, the chamber met every one of its goals including obtaining the most memberships in its 125-year history, the highest rating of membership satisfaction, a budget surplus, accreditation for the first time by the U.S. Chamber of Commerce and recognition as the areas major force in economic development.

Much of the credit goes to my Visible Strategy storyboard process. Every decision related to the chamber's strategic plan was documented and tracked to completion on a visual display. It contained names of people on the board of directors or on committees who were responsible for specific action strategies, noted a target date for completion and recorded actual date of completion. It worked as a subtle motivator for people to complete an assignment because their name is attached to it for all to see. It emphasizes accountability.

Two other steps I took at the chamber also had long-lasting impact. I initiated the Spirit of Saginaw award to be given to a man and a woman in the community who made the most difference as a volunteer during the past year. And I conducted the first ever Education and Business Day whereby students spent the day as interns with area business leaders. Both activities continue at the present time. These were symbolic actions taken to focus attention on issues important to the organization and the community.

Whatever the situation or the issue, or the organization and its size, or the people involved, SCM provides the means to get the right message to the right people at the right time through the right channels. As a stand alone mechanism to shape change for the better and get meaningful results, it is unexcelled.

4

HOW THE CONCEPT EVOLVED

Starting over 50 years ago with first job as teen-ager,
then with General Motors

Although organizational communications is a fragmented and nebulous process, most of which is essentially one-way and initiated by the organization's hierarchy, there are some generally accepted effective practices, but, no distinct and specific system. And that is what I have created—a system based on tested and proven techniques that incorporates the fundamental elements of communications with one that is strategic, manageable and aimed at specific outcomes.

What follow are a discussion about how the concept of Synchronous Communications Management evolved in my mind and practice as I passed through various jobs before graduation from college and advanced from a first-line supervisor, to general supervisor, to middle management, to executive and to senior executive during 30 years, 1962-1992, at General Motors. I offer it as step-by-step experiences which became the basis for the SCM systems' rationale, substance, structure and deployment.

Beginning with my first job while a high school student, as a gas station attendant in DePue, Illinois and other jobs as a coal delivery worker, carpenter helper, floral greenhouse hand, corn detasseling inspector, union chemical manufacturing laborer, engineer assistant, union zinc refinery laborer, estate gardener, audio visual film inspector, library attendant, janitor, and inventory clerk while working my way through college, I knew what it was like to be an employee. I knew the rules of work. I was an experienced employee.

I observed, listened and learned from the employees I worked with, from steel and chemical unions leaders and from the members of management for whom I worked. And I developed a strong sensitivity about people, their interests and their values.

I heard about why unions were formed and why they are still needed. Fellow employees talked about what the organization was doing wrong and about how they were treated by their bosses. The great majority of the information we received came from the grapevine.

I had a thirst for information about my job and the organization. Usually, I had to ask for it. As I progressed from one job to the next, I mentally noted what I would do, if I were in a position of responsibility, to proactively share information with other personnel.

While in high school, I was somewhat of a social animal. I was a member of the student council, National Honor Society, Spanish club, mixed chorus, men's quartet, drama club, band, class officer and lettered in basketball and baseball. Most of these activities required meetings. Some involved discussions and decisions. I absorbed every thing I could about "organization" and the interaction of people involved in a common cause.

With this kind of background, I was comfortable in dealing with organizational and human dynamics and often wondered how I would handle being in charge.

THE GENERAL MOTORS CONNECTION STARTS AT DELCO REMY

I got my first opportunity to do that in 1962 when I graduated from the University of Illinois and was hired by GM's Delco Remy Division as a production supervisor at its headquarters in Anderson, Indiana. As a student engineer-in-training, I was impressed with the six-month orientation I received, but, disappointed, following its completion, that I had to ask for information about non-routine issues. In those days, there were only the Delco Remy tabloid and few, if any, employee meetings other than those about safety in the workplace.

Once into the job, I developed a style of communications with my boss, with my subordinates, and with my peers which included letting them know about my plans, problems, progress, and related job issues on a regular and frequent basis.

While a manufacturing supervisor, I would pass along information to my subordinates almost immediately after I received it and tried to relate the information to how it may affect them, the department or plant operations. At the start of the shift, I would assign some employees to specific jobs, review the operation with them and answer their questions. Other employees had permanent assignments. Once the shift was underway, I made the rounds to check on progress and problems and repeated that several times a day to briefly chat. Every Friday, when I passed out paychecks, I stopped long enough to have a more casual conversation with each employee.

When new employee's would come into the department by transfer or recent hire, I would ask them to sit at my desk until I oversaw shift start-up. Then I would give them an overview of the department operations, a talk about safety and take them for a tour of the plant pointing to where our departments parts originated or were used in subassemblies. Throughout this process, I asked them if they had any questions and encouraged them to ask questions and share information in the future. I was told by many employees that no one had ever done that with them before.

As a result of this procedure, I received a lot of input, including complaints and suggestions. Whenever an employee wanted to talk with me about the job, I would jot down notes on 3x5 cards that I always carried with me. This accomplished two things: it let the employee know that what was being said was important to me and it served as a reminder to me about the issue. I never failed to get back with someone who expected a later response.

Another thing I did was to use symbolism and ceremony to reinforce an issue. Having been a Cub Scout, Boy Scout and high school and college basketball player, I experienced various events, ceremonies and rituals as a means of reward and recognition for accomplishment. So, I thought why not apply them to the job.

Good housekeeping was important in the plant for safety and quality reasons. I was always assigned to machining departments where oil mist and metal shavings were a constant problem. I expected employees workplaces to be neat and clean and tried to set the example by keeping my work area orderly or by picking up a piece of trash, shop cloths or gloves left unattended. I commended employees for their efforts. And I asked janitors to give special attention in mopping areas around large equipment and authorized overtime, in certain cases, to maintain cleanliness for the next shift. The department earned the plant housekeeping award just about every month. We celebrated together. I bought coffee for everyone.

To promote quality work in the department, I conducted a Trim Defects Too campaign. To launch it, I sat and discussed defect detection and quality with each employee for ten minutes. We talked about the final product, the employees' job, the operation on the product and how to handle specific problems. Then I gave them a nail clipper on a key ring with the slogan stamped on it as a reminder. I repeated the discussion once a month about quality progress. The results were remarkable. Rework and scrap went down, the number of employee suggestions rose, and departmental efficiency and quality ratings increased.

This face-to-face contact with the people with whom I worked had a profound affect on them and me. It still has to this day and is one of the driving forces of the Synchronous Communications Management system. It was amazing how employees responded to one-on-one conversation with their supervisor. A mandatory five-minute safety talk once a month came no where close to having the impact on employees as did the quality discussion. The safety talk was more preaching while the one on quality engaged us both on the same level person-to-person.

Some of my superiors had a positive impact on me as well, particularly while I was a manufacturing supervisor. The plant assistant manager, who went on to become a GM vice president, would make the time to walk to my department and carry on a conversation with me about the operation. He sought out my opinions and always got around to topics other than work. He was a breath of fresh air and unlike the typical manager.

The divisional manufacturing director visited my department about once a month. He would ask questions about problem areas and was interested in what was being done to fix them.

These relationships added to my sense of management's communications know-how. That know-how was conspicuous by its absence in most other managers.

As a manufacturing general supervisor, communications took on a broader look. Five supervisors reported to me on each of two shifts. They oversaw a total of 300 employees.

One of my goals was to help the supervisors become better communicators. Besides daily consultation with them, I held weekly meetings, after shifts end, to share information about schedules and production issues and once a month to track budget, safety and information from the plant manager. In addition, I met once a month with each one to coach them and discuss individual issues. This gave them a better understanding of the importance of their role and took advantage of the time to get to know one another personally as well as professionally.

I also made it a point to walk around each department during the shift to observe what was going on and say "Hello" if not converse with employees along the way.

Over the course of nine years, I served in five departments as a supervisor and five areas as general supervisor. In every post, I learned more about the people—employees, management and union—and their interests in the job and the organization. It became evident to me that peoples interests about the organization were basically the same, but, their interests about the job varied according to their level in the organization. It dawned on me that people at different job levels had different information needs.

With each promotion or new assignment, I enhanced my communications and management style. Some of the improvements came from knowledge about what interested people. Others were the result of my determination of what were important and relevant relative to the people and the organization. A significant degree of that knowledge was a synergy of my management education, personal experiences and what I was learning on my own about the process of communications from employees, magazines, books and trade publications.

In 1972, I was promoted to special assignment on the division's Labor Relations Staff. This move was made in time to allow me to become familiar with the upcoming GM-United Auto Workers national contract negotiations as well as the local contract between Delco Remy and the local UAW unit. The major part of the job involved dealing with union employee grievances and resolutions.

I was assigned to investigate employee alleged contract violations by talking to the employees supervisor and union representative to obtain background information and details about the dispute. Following that, the procedure called for writing a brief, similar to a legal brief, which described the complaint and noted the contract provision associated with it.

In the course of gathering information, I became acquainted with the people involved and their interests. It became clear to me that most grievances resulted from a lack of communications or misunderstanding between the supervisor and the employee. Often the problem was triggered by the supervisor withholding information and employee retaliation for that perceived offense. I noticed that in departments where supervisors shared information, the number of formal suggestions submitted were high and the number of grievances were low, if non-existent.

Grievance negotiation and resolution were conducted at weekly meetings between members of the union shop committee and labor relations department. Unfortunately, not all grievances were settled on their own merits. Many were withdrawn by the union in exchange for other gain. By being part of these discussions, it became apparent to me that union leaders did not understand the nature of the business. Maybe they did not want to, but on the other hand, management made little attempt to share information about such issues as the cost of doing business, the link between productivity and job security and what the competition was doing.

An adversarial relationship was generally accepted as a way of life by both sides. During the time I was at Delco Remy, it was known by others in the corporation as the West Point of GM, but it was also seen as the division with the worst union-management relationship. Whether the two reputations were related is debatable.

I did not stay in labor relations long enough to try to influence any significant improvements. However, I felt that the mind-set of union leadership could have been altered to a more constructive slant by engaging its leaders in dialogue, apart from negotiations, that had the tone of a partnership and shared information. After about a year on that job, I was promoted to Delco Remy's Public Relations Staff.

My entry into the world of public relations in 1973 was a complete surprise to me because my career goals were in manufacturing management. I had aspirations to become a plant manager, division general manager, and higher. When asked if I was interested in the PR job, my response was to ask for two weeks to check out what PR was all about. I was given that time and my research proved interesting enough to encourage me to accept. I was the only person, among 270 on GM's PR staff, with an operations and labor relations background.

I later learned that I was selected for PR because I was "a good writer, a good organizer, a good communicator who gets along very well with people, including union stewards, and very effective in the community" where I was active as a Boy Scout leader, Little League Baseball manager, and Parent-Teacher Association president.

My primary job duty in PR was community relations with secondary responsibilities to assist the editor of the monthly tabloid, one the few and oldest house organs in GM at the time.

About this same period, General Motors formally established a corporate internal communication function. A position of corporate communications director was added to its Public Relations Staff with the objective to publish a corporate newsletter and encourage the thirtysome GM divisions and staffs to do the same at the local level. Emphasis was to be placed on training current employees to become editors and skillful in all the areas involved in producing the publication. Internal workshops for editors served as the major event to affect the new directive.

Although most of my time was consumed by community activities, my interest in what was going on in the division remained high. I proposed that a weekly, one-page newsletter be published for the 30,000 employees at the Indiana site and offered to edit it. My boss agreed, with the caveat that the newsletter would not go to the DR battery plants in five other states. And since there were no resources to support me, I would have to do it by myself. I told him that I understood. I was off and running in search of information about the industry and the division, information that I thought would be of value to employees and of benefit to the business.

Getting information was not easy. I had thought that because of the tabloid, story sources were already in place, but that was not the case. The tabloids' content was basically about products, suggestion and service awards, community activities, salaried employee job changes and—want ads from employees selling personal items. Not much pertained to the business and what did was after the fact.

I decided to check with friends of mine who worked in the plants and offices to find out what was going on. It was not very long before a network with them was established. This group of people became the focus group that provided me with a great deal of insight about employee information needs and issues. They also became the newsletter distribution network and my first "embedded" reporters.

Two years after I entered PR, Delco Remy top management decided to sponsor a 5am—8am radio program for Anderson employee's. The Factory Whistle Show was also geared for community consumption to support civic organizations and general topics of interest. I was given the responsibility to coordinate production of the program and counsel the radio stations on-air person.

We developed a format of music; discussion of on-the-job and off-the -job safety provided by two Delco Remy safety engineers; interviews with employees about such things as suggestion awards, product development and quality; and other topics that were upbeat and had broad appeal.

I even started a contest for the listeners that varied for each of the five-days-a- week broadcast, to increase the number of people who followed the program. A pocket-size transistor radio was the daily prize—which proved very popular and effective to expand the audience. Today, iPod message's could be sent.

My dealings with the news and trade media were also a big part of my job. This included obtaining publicity for community organizations activities as well as Delco Remy operations. As spokesperson for the division during such goings-on as labor negotiations, labor strikes, layoffs, facility expansions, and product development and manufacture, I became very conversant regarding a multitude of topics. I received an education in what interested people from the questions asked by the reporters.

During the five years as Supervisor of Public Relations at Delco Remy, I gained a reputation as a community leader who put a friendly and helpful face on the local GM operations. In each assignment, every thing I did involved improving communications with the organizations and people with whom I came in contact. It started with learning which issues were important to them, what their needs were, and what I could do to help. Usually it included getting other people engaged in the dialogue. Before long a pattern to my approach began to form. And it became a system that proved effective no matter who was involved or what was the issue.

My PR job gave me more opportunities to get a better sense regarding how people from all walks of life felt about where they worked and how they felt about their community. I was elected to the board of directors of the YMCA, Junior Achievement, the Salvation Army, the Anderson Symphony Orchestra and others. I founded the Madison County, Indiana, Historic Home Commission, served as special events chairman for the Madison County Sesquicentennial Celebration Commission and vice president of the countys' American Bicentennial Celebration Commission, was appointed to committees for the United Way, Red Cross, Urban League, Girl Scouts and was one of three persons who brought All America City honors to Anderson.

I also created a Delco Remy speakers bureau to get out the message about the American free enterprise system, about business in general, and about the Delco Remy Division. I was the main speaker, but on occasion a certain topic of expertise was requested by community groups so I scheduled a Remy top engineer or personnel executive to address them.

As a result of giving an average of three presentations a month for five years, I had the opportunity to meet with a variety of people. And the range and depth of their questions gave me a great deal of knowledge about their interests.

The county sesquicentennial celebration exposed me to the importance of meetings and events and how they were conducted. Planning started a year in advance with weekly meetings to set goals and monitor progress by reports from committee chairpersons. Among the special events I conducted, two of them utilized "celebrity"—the largest ever parade in the area was led by film and television star Dale Robertson as grand marshal and the dedication of the new county courthouse was keynoted by soon-to-be U.S. vice president Gerald Ford.

When an historic home was to be demolished to make way for a parking lot, I joined a group of citizen's to save it. I was appointed fundraising chair and conducted a telethon and other events across the county to obtain matching funds to a grant. I then became chair of the commission that I created which oversaw the homes restoration and admittance to the National Register of Historic Places.

And when the Red Cross chapter needed $100,000 to pay for a special bus which accommodated only wheel chairs, Carl Erskine, former Brooklyn Dodger pitching great, and I organized the effort. The total sum was reached in a short time due to the huge turnout to a special concert performed by the nationally known Gaithers gospel group who lived nearby. People from all areas, including churches, fire departments, law enforcement, schools, business and health care were part of this effort.

Hearing about people's interests and observing how they interact and behave at meetings and in casual conversation and social settings instilled a new level of consciousness in me. I learned a lot about how to reach people and engage them in support of an issue. And I learned a lot about community and organizational dynamics.

NEXT STOP GM'S FISHER BODY DIVISION

My accomplishments at Delco Remy Division, on a variety of projects, further enhanced my standing with corporate PR to the extent of being promoted to GM's 300,000-employee Fisher Body Division, as Administrator of PR, in Warren, Michigan in 1978.

I was selected by the Fisher Body Divisional PR director because I "got results in any endeavor... and generated substantial goodwill for GM" and Fisher Body had a long-time problem that no one had been able to solve.

Fisher Body's dilemma was a 13-year-old environmental situation at one of its 22 plants. Soot from the plant power house in Lansing, Michigan frequently doused the neighborhood surrounding the plant and harsh odor from the automobile body paint drying ovens caused outcry from people who lived nearby.

The pollution occasionally reached the state capitol and city hall which were within walking distance of the plant.

Using my mantra of right information to right audience at right time through right channels, I decided to spend one day a week in Lansing to talk to people inside and outside of the company.

I went door-to-door in the neighborhood. I introduced myself, explained that I was new to Fisher Body and asked about the soot, odor, and any other problem they had with the operation. Many people invited me into the house to talk. Several of them showed me particles of soot on window sills. Others walked me to their cars and pointed to soot on the dashboard. The mayor and a city councilman both resided in the neighborhood so I made regular visits to their offices and those of other key officials to conduct frequent dialogue.

I talked to employees—managers, production workers, engineers, power-house technicians and plant security. Before long I was known by the plant staff, the mayor, city council, state legislators, the Lansing Clean Air Commission, plant neighbors, and the media among others.

Complaints telephoned to the plant manager's office were responded to immediately by a member of plant security who went to the complainants home to verify the odors and soot presence and severity and the date and time of the event.

The toughest part of resolving the problems was determining whether the pollutants actually were coming from the plant and then convincing top management to come up with a fix. I kept a record of analysis of the soot from window sills and a log of complaints about odor. The soot was the same as that from the powerhouse and the time of paint odor complaints correlated with drying oven operation.

The next step was to report my findings to top management. The evidence was overwhelming. That did it. Top management agreed to a $1.5 million engineering fix of the power house and drying ovens.

During the subsequent two years of construction and installation of power house and oven equipment , I kept all the stakeholders informed of every step of my activities and progress. Through lunch meetings with the key people, face-to-face discussions with neighbors, letters to various stakeholders and statements to the media, I responded to every question and complaint no matter who the source.

Several plant neighbors claimed that discharges from the power house had caused damage to siding on their house and to paint on their cars and trucks, so I called on outside environmental engineers to inspect them. No connection was found with the plant, but the neighbors were appreciative of our concern and effort.

By this time, the goodwill generated as a result of our timely and frequent discussions with stakeholders took our relationship to a new level. The feelings of hostility and frustration that prevailed during the previous 13 years turned into a sense of amiability and cooperative attitude. People trusted us because they saw we were open, honest, responsive and sincerely interested in stopping the pollution.

The third year of my tenure at Fisher Body the project was completed. The problems were eliminated by the addition of ductwork from the paint ovens to the powerhouse to incinerate paint spray, a new 250-foot smokestack to disperse fumes away from the neighborhood and a huge sheetmetal device, designed by Fisher Body engineers, that extracted soot from the system before it was discharged into the air.

An open house of the plant, with stakeholders as guests of honor, was held to celebrate the accomplishment. Neighbors and their families and civic leaders were bussed to the plant where they were given tours of the reengineered power house and paint ovens. Refreshments were served and plant staff gave presentations explaining facility improvements. Employees were especially appreciative for being involved in the project and for the manner in which they were kept informed.

The Lansing State Journal carried an editorial the next day commending Fisher Body for its outstanding corporate citizenship.

Two months later I appeared before the Lansing city council to request a $50 million tax abatement for a multimillion-dollar investment in additional plant facilities which would create new jobs. The council unanimously approved the request. It was generally acknowledged that the abatement would have been denied if Fisher Body had allowed the pollution situation to continue.

The soot collection device was so effective that GM decided to offer its unique design for use in similar non-GM coal-fired powerhouses throughout the United States. I spearheaded the announcement of the technology and conducted major news conferences in Washington D.C. with the U.S. Environmental Protection Agency and in Columbus, Ohio with the Ohio EPA. GM received numerous accolades for the gesture from a variety of organizations and individuals.

My pattern for effective communication worked again. This time the stakeholder input and management's receptiveness increased in importance, in my mind, along with my role as proactive liaison and coordinator of information flow. I knew that if dialogue could be generated, common ground would be found and understanding and achievement would occur. A win-win situation would result.

My evaluation of why the situation went on for 13 years is that no one at Fisher Body or General Motors thought to take a proactive and interactive approach in addressing the issue. GM's prior emphasis was more a matter of recording complaints and filing internal reports. No one recognized that defining the issue, obtaining relevant information and sharing it in a coordinated fashion with the key parties involved was part of the solution. Dealing directly with the various audiences was apparently not a major consideration.

Communications management also played a valuable role internally in my second year at Fisher Body. GM had just established a political action committee which accepted contributions for candidates for office and political parties from certain managers and executives. This was of great interest to me so I educated myself about the who, what, when, why, where, and how of the PAC. I decided that someone should coordinate this at the division. I put my ideas into the form of a proposal and volunteered. I was named Administrator of PR and Governmental Affairs.

The next thing I did was to edit a monthly newsletter about the PAC and political issues facing GM and the industry. I scheduled and coordinated quarterly meetings for eligible staff at headquarters and made the rounds of the 22 Fisher Body plants to promote the PAC to eligible staff at those sites. Elected officials were invited to address the groups including U.S. senators and congressmen and state legislators from the five states where Fisher Body had operations. Local officials were also included in the meetings.

Both the newsletter and meetings kept PAC activities and industry issues visible to manager's and executive's. They were subtly educated about the benefits of their contributions to GM and about legislation affecting the auto industry. And they became more engaged in the political process by writing letters to those officials, telephoning them and tracking legislation.

Fisher Body contributions to the PAC rose to those among the highest in GM. The communications process got the job done again.

A third major achievement, which had no connection to my job description, was the establishment of employee newsletters at each of the 22 Fisher Body plants. I talked to employees at every level when visiting plants and concluded that very little information was being shared on a regular basis. I was able to persuade plant managers to appoint a salaried employee, usually, the managers secretary, to work with me and initiate a monthly publication.

Within my first year , the number of newsletters went from four to 22. Not only did this conform to the GM corporate objective, it gave plant management, union leaders, and hourly and salaried employees a springboard from which to start more relevant dialogue about plant business topics. Newsletters dovetailed at that time with GM's new Quality of Work Life program with the United Auto Workers which led to the GM-UAW Quality Network a decade later.

Newsletter content was a big issue at first because managers were not comfortable sharing the kind of business information of interest to plant employees. Gradually, with my insistence, information about future plans, progress of projects, cost data, and quality issues became commonplace.

Employee suggestions and suggestion awards increased due to widespread awareness of cost problems and quality requirements. Employees became more willing to share ideas with plant management and management was more receptive to consider them.

The importance of the immediate supervisor to the communications process became apparent to me about this time. It started with comments I overheard from a newly appointed plant manager at the Fleetwood plant in Detroit. An employee was describing a long standing problem at the plant and complaining that no one would listen to him and look into the situation. I heard the manager say, "Tell me, I'll listen."

Afterwards, I suggested to the manager that a "Tell me, I'll listen" campaign be conducted to encourage employees to share ideas and problems and encourage supervisors to be more responsive. By his example, he could promote communications improvement as an issue vital to plant efficiency. He told me to go ahead with it.

Supervisors were trained to prepare them to properly handle such discussions and were issued clip-on badges imprinted with "Tell me, I'll listen" to display their commitment. The plant newsletter promoted the progress of the campaign and soon other plants were picking-up on the concept.

Another thing happened which reinforced the value of symbolism and ceremony. The general manager of Fisher Body established a quality improvement award to recognize plant employees at sites where significant progress was made. He and the divisional executive staff visited plants on a quarterly basis to celebrate and present the awards. This award and the activities surrounding its achievement provided much fodder for dialogue in the plant and the plant newsletter. A reception was held for plant employees which gave top management the opportunity to meet and talk with employees on a more casual basis.

Their visibility at the plants was so well received that regular executive visits were scheduled just to review progress and meet with employees.

Product quality, teamwork, cost reduction, and customer service all took a leap forward because plant management and the workforce were sharing relevant information and were focused and engaged on achieving common objectives. The newsletters and supervisors helped to create and sustain that focus.

Another achievement, of a personal nature, was attained while I was at Fisher Body. I earned accreditation from the Public Relations Society of America during my first year of eligibility—five years of experience as a practitioner. I passed the eight-hour accreditation exam on the first try and was elated to be considered a public relations professional. More importantly, I had acquired a great deal of formal knowledge about the principles of effective public relations. This knowledge, coupled with my management expertise, gave me the courage to start to shape a focused, measured, and sustainable communications management system.

THEN, ONWARD TO GM'S SAGINAW STEERING GEAR DIVISION

In 1981, almost three years to the month from my joining Fisher Body, I was promoted to Director of Public Affairs, of what was then, GM's Saginaw Steering Gear Division, in Saginaw, Michigan. I was rewarded for not only "resolving the 13-year-old pollution problem and obtaining a $50 million tax abatement," but, "for the internal communications system and PAC program" I established at Fisher Body's 22 plants.

The opportunity was now mine at Saginaw Steering Gear to provide the leadership necessary to fully develop, implement and test my communications management system.

5

DEVELOPING A MANAGEABLE FORMAT

Putting ideas into practice when promoted
to GM communication executive

Since my early days as a part time employee and then as person who super-vised others, communications had been part of my persona. And as I de-veloped a style of communications, got results in a variety of endeavors, and saw my career advance, I realized that there was a pattern and framework to what I was doing. The next step was to put it into a manageable format.

So, here was my chance, as Saginaw Steering Gear Director of Public Af-fairs, to bring all my communications and management practices together into a single system—a proactive approach to an interactive process which facili-tates the sharing of information across the organization.

It has been my belief for a long time that where there is dialogue—talking and listening—and shared information among people, sooner than later com-mon ground will be found and progress will occur because everyone has a voice that is heard. After all, information is power and people feel empowered and trusted with it. Only then are they willing to trust, commit and give discre-tionary effort—effort which is above and beyond the call—to the cause.

My vision was to establish a coordinated process of planning, organizing, directing and monitoring which gets the right information to the right audience at the right time by the right channels and creates awareness, understanding, acceptance and support.

Initial objectives included:

• Educate executive staff members on what internal communications can accomplish in term of bottom line results to institutionalize the process.

- Strengthen print communications by increasing business news in the daily *Newsletter* to at least 75 percent of total content, initiate a monthly tabloid to provide more in-depth business information, publish special newsletters for other key stakeholders such as employee's immediate supervisor and company suppliers.
- Increase face-to-face dialogue among management, supervisors and employees at every level.
- Audit, evaluate and fine tune the communications process on a regular basis.

I realized that everything I wanted to accomplish might not happen in the ideal sequence. The important thing was to do what would be effective and get meaningful results, then build on that success to get to the next plane. Furthermore, I decided that whatever is done must align with the organization's vision and strategic direction.

One of my first priorities at Saginaw was to audit the status of the current internal communications process to determine its strengths and weaknesses and employee perceptions of the flow of information downward, upward, and laterally. A survey of the 30,000 employees found: a lack of trust between management and the workforce, little information sharing about plans, information was not timely, minimum employee involvement, inconsistent management practices, the grapevine as the main source of information, supervisors were the preferred source, middle management received information at the same time or after union leaders and supervisors basically received little more than production schedules and safety information.

Since downward communication was sorely lacking, the first things I did to improve communications were to publish a quarterly tabloid that would complement an existing daily, one page newsletter and increase newsletter divisional information to a minimum of 75 percent of total content. Too many of the previous articles were not relevant to the business nor pertinent to all hourly and salaried employees.

The tabloid would provide the means for management to speak with one voice to the entire division and give more in-depth information about divisional issues and plans. An employee contest was held to name it. *Steering Columns* became so popular that monthly publication became necessary to demonstrate management's' commitment to communications improvement. Employees wanted more information and wanted it more often. The tabloid also became acclaimed as the official and reliable origin for just about every kind of information that was not proprietary or confidential. And people looked for it as a regular and frequent source of truthful and meaningful information.

By sticking to business topics and cross-promoting the tabloid with the newsletter and vice versa, the articles in both publications took on new relevancy, consistency, importance and timeliness as issues from the divisional plan were addressed, explored and explained. To ensure there was 100 percent receipt of the tabloid, it was mailed to employee homes at all sites. The newsletter continued to be faxed to locations outside of Saginaw where it was handed-out or posted at specified places inside the facilities.

A tickler-file calendar was designed for the tabloid so that certain topics like quality improvement, cost reduction, teamwork and customer satisfaction would appear in every issue while others were scheduled to appear a prescribed number of times less often.

The newsletter continued to be the channel for daily information. In case of urgent and critical information and significant events, the breaking news was put out immediately in a special edition of the newsletter.

To handle news gathering, plant and office reporters where recruited from those staffs and persons in my department were assigned as liaison with them. Before long, the plant reporters became plant newsletter editors and office reporters became editors who published a monthly publication about staff department activities.

This "embedding" of news sources served as spokes of a wheel of information feeding into the communications department as the hub. It served to strengthen lateral communications and provide relevant information on a timely basis. And it helped to build a better understanding about every departments role and the value of collaboration.

Everything of significance that happened or was going on in any unit was quickly brought to the attention of a communications manager. When a quality problem was avoided or resolved, a story ran in the divisional newsletter describing the situation and fix. Some of the more notable solutions appeared in a tabloid article.

The divisional general manager wrote personal letters to the people involved in improving quality, thanking and commending them for their alertness and ideas. He said he read about it in the newsletter. What a tremendously positive impact that had on employees. Word spread across the plant and division that people were being heard and recognized for ideas to help the business and that the top boss found out about it in the newsletter.

Simultaneous to these activities, I began to educate the general manager and my colleagues on the executive staff about what good internal communications could accomplish. I circulated select magazines, journals and articles that described these activities, as well as the reasons for their success or failure, in other business organizations. I knew if they saw that communications management contributed to the bottom line and added value to the relationship with the workforce, there would be unanimous support to expand the system.

And that is what happened. The number of persons on my staff went from three to 12 as each major segment of the communications system was added and put into effect. Included were a communications manager at each manufacturing site outside of Michigan and one in Europe.

In an earlier audit, members of middle management indicated an inadequate amount of timely information was reaching them. They felt out of the loop. More often than not, union leaders got information first from labor relations. To correct that, I promoted a policy stipulating middle management as the primary audience to receive official information followed by supervisors and, simultaneously, union leaders and hourly and salaried employees.

In addition, I proposed the first in a calendar of required meetings be mandated for middle management. Meetings by conference call with each outlying site, chaired by the general manager, were scheduled every month to share financial information, product quality reports, and other performance benchmarks. Other executives also attended the sessions which always concluded with a questions and answers segment. This opened up a new meaning to information sharing.

Supervisors were next in line for attention. Their response to the audit revealed a huge information gap except for production schedules and safety promotion. Two improvements were made immediately. A monthly meeting between the supervisor's and their immediate supervisor was decreed and a bimonthly newsletter *Report to Supervisors* initiated. This two-page newsletter contained advance business information to be used in discussions with subordinates and tips for self-improvement and effective management techniques.

With the establishment of plant and department reporters, plant editors and plant and department newsletters, a demand for communications with this group of people was generated. Workshops for editor training and quarterly meetings with editors and reporters continued to strengthen and reinforce the focus on divisional and departmental performance targets.

This was further enhanced with the addition of a newsletter for those persons who coordinated the process. *Dialog* was filled with writing and editing tips, story ideas, interviewing techniques and other professional areas of inter-est which helped broaden editors expertise. The publication broadened editors perspective beyond the plant newsletter to a greater understanding of internal communications. It created new dynamics in employee communications and brought a strong sense of purpose and connection.

ENGAGING THE GENERAL MANAGER AND EXECUTIVE STAFF

About two years into my job at Saginaw, I took what was probably the most important step in establishing communications as a invaluable activity, one that would engage the leadership and institutionalize the process. I formed and chaired the Communications Review Group comprised of the general manager and the executive staff.

The group, which met monthly, was an after-the- fact -body whose role was to review employee communications activities, including survey results and dis-tribution methods, provide constructive criticism, and suggest topic and story ideas of importance to the division. It was not an editorial panel. This accom-plished two vital objectives: top management set the example by getting per-sonally involved in and actively supporting the communications management process, and top management devoted regular attention to communications as a key organizational function.

The group, unique in General Motors and perhaps among American corpo-rations, became the inspiration behind the development of the internal com-munications plan which included a vision statement, a mission statement, a philosophy statement, objectives and definition of specific communication products and events. The plan was enthusiastically endorsed because it defined the purpose, goals and objectives of the function and gave legitimacy and value to its existence. It also continued to keep expectations of the process high.

Saginaw Steering Gear's internal communications Vision Statement stated "Every employee is aware of, understands, accepts and supports the goals and objectives of the division and takes action to achieve them individually and col-laboratively."

The Mission Statement of the Communications Department read "In the interests of Saginaw Steering Gear Division and its people, we will function as advocates of employee awareness, understanding, acceptance and support of divisional goals and objectives by providing open, accurate, and timely information in a climate of mutual respect. To accomplish this mission, we will provide the planning, implementation and coordination for sharing relevant information downward, upward and laterally; training; research; guidelines; counsel and a means to measure the effectiveness of specific communications efforts."

To increase awareness concerning what communications was all about and set the tone for everyone's part, the Philosophy Statement was phrased this way:

"It is Saginaw Steering Gear Division's intent to communicate with all employees on subjects important to them and to the division. Basic to this climate is an open flow of information downward, upward and laterally throughout the division so that employees can understand divisional objectives and feel free to express their ideas and concerns.

While the divisions top management is responsible for overall leadership in encouraging, maintaining and enhancing a communications-oriented climate throughout the division, all immediate supervisors are responsible for ownership of the communications process. They are responsible for keeping communications lines open between themselves and employees they supervise and for communicating with these employees in accordance with divisional objectives. The employees immediate supervisor is responsible as the primary link in the communications process.

In addition, all employees are encouraged to communicate with their supervisors and other employees in a cooperative manner on work-related matters and provide information that may aid in accomplishing their responsibilities and organizational goals.

Management will make every effort to tell the bad news along with the good, provide information to employees no later than its release to the public whenever possible and provide immediate supervisors with the tools and training necessary to become effective communicators."

The communications improvements made substantial changes for the better in the organizational culture. However, they were essentially informing people and not creating the opportunity for dialogue—the give and take—I felt was necessary to strengthen the bond and collaboration between employees and their supervisor and among fellow employees.

What I did next was to create what became the single most effective subsystem of all—a video newsmagazine. Video was chosen because I thought it a more credible medium than print and the information could be seen and heard coming from real people. *Perspective* was a bimonthly, 20-minute program which was shown to all employees, on company time, by the immediate supervisors as part of a regular monthly meeting with their respective employee group.

The meeting was a powerful event because it created a forum for information sharing and focused supervisor and employee on a key business issue. Only relevant and sometimes confidential information was presented and it gave them the opportunity to discuss and relate it to their particular department or function. In short, the meeting created meaningful face-to-face dialogue downward, upward, and laterally among participants.

Each program was written and produced in house, although an outside TV personality was hired to serve as anchor and narrator. The program manager, a member of the communications staff, served as producer, writer, interviewer, director and editor. He was also responsible for a leaders guide to help the immediate supervisor set the stage for the program, lead the discussion and handle questions following the viewing. And he tracked and documented that meetings were actually held and recorded employee evaluations of the program and the supervisor's meeting effectiveness. The latter led to meeting effectiveness training for supervisors while the former provided feedback on improvements for future programs.

Interviews with hourly and salaried employees, executives, managers, first-line supervisors, union leaders, customers, and suppliers were presented so that both sides to an issue could be told or to get information about the topic from the persons closest to it who were most knowledgeable.

At first employees could not believe that they were to be given company time to attend a meeting to view a video and talk about it with their supervisor. From the initial program on, it was obvious to them that management was sincere and serious about increasing information sharing. It was also apparent that what they were reading in the tabloid and newsletter and hearing from their supervisor was factual and not fluff.

And they responded accordingly. The trust level measurements between management and employees jumped to higher plateaus into the 80 percentile. So did the number of suggestions and suggestion awards—from an average of $864 up to $5748 in a six-year period.

Meetings took on new a importance not only in my mind, but, in the minds of the other top executives. Those views were reinforced when I suggested the general manager meet with groups of hourly and salaried employees on a regular basis. No one would have more impact on them than the top boss of the division, I advised.

So a "no holds barred" one-hour session with a large group of hourly employees and one with salaried employees were scheduled for him at a Saginaw, Michigan plant to test the concept. Plant management or department heads were not invited. The general manager started the meetings by giving a brief state of the business report and then asked for questions and comments. Two and one-half hours later the meeting ended, but not before employees had a chance to voice complaints, suggestions, and ask a host of questions for which they got specific answers or a promise that he would look into the situation.

The employees were wowed by his openness and candidness, not to mention the fact he spent so much time with them. The general manager was so impressed with the high interest of the groups and the number of knowledgeable questions and comments that he agreed to continue employee meetings once a month at a plant or staff location divisionwide.

As a result of this success, I developed a calendar of meetings that would mandate face-to-face dialogue between management and hourly and salaried employees and took it to the executive staff for agreement and commitment. They did both even though it meant taking people away from their jobs.

Just about every possible interface was considered, 19 sessions in all:

FACE-TO-FACE MEETING CALENDAR

Daily Start of Workday Meetings
   Immediate Supervisor, Workgroup

Weekly Executive Staff Meeting
   General Manager, Executive Staff

Weekly Staff Head Meeting
   Staff Head, Immediate Staff Members

Weekly Joint Activities Meeting
   Site Operations Managers, Plant Managers,
   Union Representatives

Monthly General Manager/Plant Employee Meeting
    General Manager, Business Unit Director, Plant Employees
        Plant 1 July
        Plant 2 August
        Plant 3 September
        Plant 4 October
        Plant 5 November
        Plant 6 December
        Plant 7 January
        Alabama Plants February
        Buffalo Plants November
        Detroit Plants May
        Headquarters March

Monthly Plant Management Meeting
    Plant Manager, All Supervisors

Monthly Plant Manager/Employee Meeting
    Plant Manager, Hourly and Salaried Employees

Monthly Middle Management Meeting
    Executives, Managers
    All Domestic Sites Via Conference Call

Monthly Departmental Meeting
    Supervisor, Hourly Employees

Monthly Departmental Meeting
    Supervisor, Salaried Employees

Monthly Communications Review Group Meeting
    General Manager, Executive Staff

Triennial Executive Conference
    All Executives

Annual Middle Management Conference
    All Managers From All Sites

Annual First-Line Supervisors Conference
    All First-Line Supervisors at Each Site

Annual Joint Leadership Conference
    General Manager, Executive Staff, Plant Managers,
    Union Leaders From All Sites

Annual Business Unit Director/Supervisors Meeting
    Business Unit Director, Operations Manager, Supervisors

Annual State of the Division Meeting
    General Manager, Executive Staff on Video for Each Site

Annual State of the Staff Meeting
    Staff Head, Salaried Employees

Annual State of the Plant Meeting
    Plant Manager, Hourly and Salaried Employees

I also created an agenda for specific meetings as a guideline so that certain information was passed along to employees at every meeting and time was given to them for discussion, information sharing and questions:

GENERIC AGENDA

- Purpose of meeting, issues today
- Strategic plan status
- Tactical plan status
- Budget, productivity, cost, quality status
- Projects status, safety, quality
- Previous meeting decisions
- Round table discussion of general issues
- Agenda, date for next meeting
- Who else needs to know what was discussed/ decided (editor, employees, supervisor, management, others)

The printed word, video and face-to-face meetings became the three primary channels of communication. Whenever a new issue emerged, a mini plan was devised by my staff to get the right information to the right employees at the right time and frequency through one of these modes. Information flowed like never before and teamwork, productivity and profitability rose with it.

Communications measurements were a continuous process, as well, whether it was face-to-face meetings and video effectiveness evaluations, Communications Review Group feedback or plant reporter input telling us what was working or which issues interested employees. Every other year a communications audit was conducted by which we learned about employees expectations for information about the business before things happened, while things happened and after things happened.

The outside consultant who administered the survey was "amazed with the degree of credibility accorded these formal communications media."

"Most other organizations we are familiar with don't approach the high numbers we see here. What it tells us is that employees are hearing what you tell them and say they want more of it," the consultant reported.

Those words were music to my ears and they made a strong impression on my colleagues, too. From this I discovered that quantifying communications results put its value in terms top management understood—numbers. It also made it easier to get approval to expand communications activities and add the people to do the job.

MEETING THE FATHER OF PUBLIC RELATIONS

In 1984, I had the privilege of attending a two-day seminar in New York City with 93-year-old Edward Bernays who many considered to be the father of public relations. He was a wealth of information. I was in awe of his sharp mind and insights and surprised by the fact he conducted the seminar by himself. There were no assistants with him.

Bernays emphasized that his counsel was focused on the communications between an organization and its audiences whereby he communicated the organizations interest to the audience as well as the audiences interest to the organization.

He maintained that the greatest asset of the professional communicator is knowledge of applied psychology, sociology, history and economics.

"Anticipating and interpreting the publics desires and wants to management will demand a highly specialized competence that differs from other management functions," he said. "They should be people with creative minds, not necessarily good writers."

The profession, said Bernays, should be one which advises a unit on how best to achieve its goals. As an advisory function, it should act as an applied social scientist counseling on the attitudes and behavior of management in order to win favor by action, by education, by persuasion and by information to the audience concerned.

Bernays' emphasis on research to resolve any issue fascinated me to the point that I decided to investigate a question of communications that always intrigued me. That question was "How did information flow daily through an organization?" Surveys told us if employees received information and from whom, but not much was known about where there were bottlenecks. I was concerned that certain information discussed at an executive staff meeting was not being shared with lower levels nor across the three shifts of the plant operations. I also wondered how much critical information was held at lower levels and not passed up to top management. So, I decided to have my staff investigate by considering each level as an audience—executives, managers, first-line supervisors, hourly employees and salaried employees.

The study was to be conducted for a period of three months. Randomly selected employees representing each level of the division were interviewed to determine how business-related information is transmitted through the organization, how information is filtered along the way and what barriers impeded face-to-face communication.

Information flow tracking started with the weekly divisional executive staff meeting. Select data was then followed to the weekly business unit meetings, weekly plant manager-plant staff meetings, superintendent-supervisor sessions, and then to departmental meetings held between first-line supervisors and hourly and salaried employees.

Three major findings of the study were that supervisors at all levels were frequently tied up in meetings unrelated to the meetings calendar, were difficult to reach and did not have the time to transmit information. Secondly, poor communications between shifts was a major concern among first line supervisors, superintendents and plant managers because it prevented operations from running smoothly. Thirdly, hourly employees desired more information from their supervisors concerning the state of the business, but they believed supervisors gave them all the information they had.

The study noted that the high level of activity at manufacturing plants often prevented superintendents and first-line supervisors from communicating more effectively with each other.

"I feel myself being rushed and sometimes find myself trying to doing several things at once. We need to stop what we are doing and listen more to people," were comments echoed by many superintendents.

Overall, superintendents interviewed for the study agreed that they need to be more accessible to supervisors to share information and answer questions raised.

Regular face-to-face meetings between supervisors and employees in their department were judged—by participants in the study and in most other employee communications surveys—as the most effective way to share business information.

Supervisors and employees who participate in such meetings said that they find them very useful, but meetings need to more organized, held frequently and on a regular basis with adequate time given for employee questions and discussions.

Study results and updates on planned improvements were shared with employees in the monthly tabloid *Steering Columns* and daily *Newsletter*.

Our response to the study was to increase the amount of this information in the daily newsletter and tabloid, inform all supervisors at every level what employees desired and developed a special communications training program which included a module about communications management from a divisional and plant/staff standpoint. The change in their performance was enormous and well received by a huge majority of employees. Every person who supervised the efforts of others now knew what effective communication was all about and what was expected of them in sharing relevant information. Supervisors put their knowledge into practice and employees reciprocated in the spirit of the divisional communications philosophy.

The information flow study results reminded me of my years as a manufacturing supervisor and general supervisor. Sometimes the hectic pace of production made me lose sight of the human element and forget to keep people posted or even to say "Hello" to them. But those times were few because I knew how important it was to me to hear from my boss.

On the other hand, the flow study convinced me that the supervisor's role in communications will always be restricted to some degree, therefore, the communications manager must compensate for that factor by designing other avenues to ensure that the right information gets to the right employee at the right time. And, the way to do that is to incorporate it in the system as a redundant channel. In other words, accept the fact that supervisors can only receive and disseminate so much information. For every major issue, construct a back-up channel for that information. The communications staff was the back-up channel as well as the primary one.

The division was on a positive roll that continued to gain momentum. Information sharing was producing one success after the other, with management's proactive leadership setting the example and men and women in every sector of the organization responding and fulfilling their part in the process. That is not to say 100 % of employees was committed, but support and participation reached critical mass of 85%.

SHARING RELEVANT HUMOR, EDITORIAL CARTOON INTRODUCED

During this same period of time, a new feature was added to the monthly tabloid—an editorial cartoon. The idea for this "innovation" came as a result of a plant newsletter cartoon, that appeared regularly, drawn by an hourly employee. The cartoon gained a following which included the divisions' chief financial officer.

The CFO supported my suggestion to make the editorial cartoon one of the channels of information. Humor makes people think and a management that has a sense of humor is seen as more human. So, after discussion with and approval by union leaders and top management, the illustrator was added to the division's Public Relations Staff where he assumed duties for the cartoon and other communications management responsibilities.

The cartoon depicted issues and everyday occurrences familiar to Saginaw employees though the eyes of two characters affectionately known as Shopus Ratus, who represented labor, and Fatus Catus, who represented management. It soon became one of the highest rated columns for its insights, reminders and observations of company behavior and performance.

Some of the cartoons are shown in the Appendix:

- The first cartoon—A star is born...
- The synchronous manufacturing process
- The grapevine

- The journey to world class
- Globalization
- Keep the competition down
- Divisional costs
- Customer satisfaction
- Competitive prices
- World class elements
- The competitive edge
- Cost reduction

I continued to regularly scan journals, newspapers, books and magazines about communications, leadership and organizational behavior and circulate key excerpts to the executive staff. A new issue that kept cropping up caught my eye and I quickly became fascinated with it. The term "culture" was becoming a buzzword in the corporate world.

As with communications and measuring the flow of relevant information, I thought the same approach could be used for culture. Surveys are taken of customers to determine their perceptions and expectations of product quality, so why not ask employees about what they think is expected of them by the organization and their beliefs about in-house quality performance and leadership behavior. Knowing that the way people think about an issue is reflected in their behavior and identifying the way employees see the current culture's strengths and weaknesses, steps could be taken to address them.

TO UNDERSTAND NORMS AND VALUES—A CULTURE SURVEY TAKEN

My idea was to survey employees at the same five levels that were used for communications—executives, managers, first-line supervisors, hourly employees and salaried employees—to define Saginaw's Quality Culture.

I made a proposal to members of top management and suggested that union leaders at the four domestic sites be invited to participate in the survey and jointly administer it. They consented and I retained an outside national consultant to assist me in designing a survey that would measure employee commitment and define their beliefs and perceptions about their jobs, the divisions quality process and practices, the organization and management's leadership.

About 5,200 employees were polled, on the job, by a union/management team in Buffalo, New York, Athens, Alabama, and Detroit and Saginaw, Michigan.

The findings showed a mixed commitment to both the organization and quality. As we expected, management ranked highest in commitment to quality and hourly employees lowest. The hourly felt that management demanded quantity rather than quality. To our surprise, hourly employee commitment to the organization was just below management's and above that of certain groups of salaried employees.

Eighty-two percent of respondents divisionwide said "they would go out of their way to do a good job for Saginaw," and 72 percent said they are "proud of the products they help make for Saginaw."

A major conclusion of the study report was that the hourly group saw no quality improvement plan in place and a management that was out of touch with employees on quality. There was a strong perception that quantity was more important than quality. This could be reversed if top management: had a more detailed and comprehensive plan, communicated a sharper image of how to achieve conformance to requirements to middle management, directed middle management to take a more active role to translate the quality principles into everyday practices by working with supervisors to address obstacles to quality and build teamwork, encouraged more union and hourly participation and correlated quality to job security.

Recommendations to address salaried non-supervisory employees included integrating them into the concept of the quality culture through improved supervisory communications around how to pursue quality improvement in their non-manufacturing job.

As a result, the general manager appointed a task force to oversee adoption and implementation of the recommendations. In addition, communications managers took steps to provide more information on quality, costs and competitive issues to all employees which opened another new dimension of communications.

By plugging into the beliefs and expectations that shape employee behavior, new insights were obtained about how they perceive the organization and its leadership. This information was invaluable in communications development because it served as another benchmark by which to measure communications effectiveness and organizational achievement.

The division was on another roll. That is not to say there were no problems. There were and challenges, too. But, the enthusiasm and teamwork generated by sharing information, listening to employees and taking action accordingly had raised divisional performance to a new plateau. Now it was up to communicators to continuously oversee and fine-tune the process and keep up with the rapid pace of change and new issues. Management's expectations of the communications department rose, too.

To address that, it became a matter introducing new success stories and reframing information about quality into the internal communications process. Encouraging and highlighting effective management behavior to set the example for the new quality culture eventually led to a new key management objective—"Enhance Management Style.

The systems content for what became Synchronous Communications Management was essentially complete. The challenge now was to work it on a day-to-day basis. Chapter 7 covers this activity in more detail.

COMMUNITY PROJECTS ENHANCE LABOR RELATIONS

During the seven years at Saginaw Division, I was also very active in the community by my choice. I took the time to get around the community, meet people and identify community needs. This experience gave me additional knowledge about people from various sectors of the region.

During the early 1980's, businesses were closing or moving out of the city and jobs were being lost. Business people blamed the situation on unions in the area for the high wages and lack of cooperation to remain competitive. I thought that if unions were part of the problem, then they should become part of the solution. I shared my thinking on the issue with my boss, Blair Thompson, the general manager. We agreed to form The Business-Union-Government (BUG) Group for Economic Development and bring together leaders from these areas to discuss and decide how to retain and attract business and jobs.

Two leaders from each of the three groups were invited to serve as a steering committee and conduct monthly meetings with 150 other leaders to discuss how to address the situation. It took a year of meetings to produce it first successful job attraction, but the group was the catalyst for the formation of Saginaw Future—the countywide economic development agency which is now among the top units in Michigan.

The two of us also cofounded, with a Black and a Hispanic civic leader, The Saginaw Black Leadership Group and The Saginaw Hispanic Leadership

Group, respectively. We met with each group of 12 members monthly and separately so that individual issues specific to the group could be addressed.

The groups were formed to bring more minorities into mainstream community activities. Once a year we hosted a reception for the groups members and spouses to get together for fellowship. We made history by having it in our homes.

The main interest of the Hispanics was education and reducing the drop-out rate of Hispanic high school students. Black leaders wanted to concentrate on creating minority-owned businesses and train minority managers. The Saginaw superintendent of schools was invited to the Hispanic group meeting and a special program, which is still active, was established in the school district to assist Hispanic students. A Black-owned corporation was formed after the group obtained a contract from Saginaw Division to rebuild automotive hydraulic power steering pumps.

All of the above activities involved hourly and salaried GM employees which enhanced labor relations.

Blair Thompson was a very willing participant in community affairs and gave several key speeches to civic groups every year. In the short time before he was promoted to GM group vice president to organize the Automotive Components Group (now Delphi), he was recognized as the top business leader in the county.

When Mark McCabe became general manager, he and I founded Leadership Saginaw which provided training to future civic leaders. He, too, was involved in the community and in one of his speeches about leadership to a service club, he suggested training interested citizens in those skills. The response to it was overwhelming. The local newspaper published an editorial supporting the idea. Leadership Saginaw is still active today under the Saginaw County Chamber of Commerce.

In addition to those activities, I got to know more about the human condition and peoples interests by serving on the board of directors of the Red Cross, Junior Achievement, the Saginaw County Growth Alliance, the Tri-County Private Industry Council and the Governor of Michigan's Task Force on Airline Transportation.

Due to the strong support of three general managers—the late Ellis Ivey, who brought me to Saginaw Division and approved publication of the tabloid, W. Blair Thompson, who gave me great freedom and support in internal communications and community relations, and Mark McCabe, who continued that free-rein and expanded communication's influence inside the division, and colleagues on the executive staff, who in a short time grasped the value of this activity—communications management was put on par with the other departmental functions. No other GM division could say the same.

6

TRANSFORMING THE FORMAT INTO A SYSTEMS MODEL AND REFINING IT

Composing and implementing
Synchronous Communications Management

Another promotion was given to me in 1988. GM had named a new group vice president to consolidate its 15 component divisions and 300,000 employees under the name of the Automotive Components Group (ACG). This was the front-runner to what is now Delphi Corporation. I became its first Group Director of Communications and Public Affairs.

It was my job to assist in planning the consolidation and in managing the unit with the other ACG executive staff members while leading the 15 divisional communications and public affairs directors and their staffs to keep employees and other stakeholders worldwide informed about the changes, plans, progress and business.

My first act was to schedule monthly meetings with the public affairs directors to develop a communications plan framework. Teams were established to address important issues surrounding the communications function and the consolidation and make recommendations for action.

As I deliberated about how to bring together 90 communications professionals and 15 communications structures under one banner, it occurred to me that the Synchronous Communications Management system was just the thing to help facilitate it. First, I would have to give the 15 directors and my immediate staff of four professionals some training in the system so that we would be of the same mind-set and have the same understanding about it. But, before the training, I would have to develop a layout of the model on paper and determine the support material needed to explain it. The end-product of the training would be the communications plan framework, for the ACG, that each division would adopt and implement in line with its particular strategic business plan.

My thoughts went back to the seminar with Edward Bernays when he laid-out his eight-step process for helping clients meet their goals. It contained the principles of his "engineering of consent" which included conducting audience research, modification of goals, setting strategies, themes and slogans, and timing of tactics. The keys to success were attitudes and actions that speak louder than words.

This brought a new dimension to my thinking for the development of the Synchronous Communications model, one that brought to mind the need for illustrations that depict the interrelationship of its elements and a worksheet requiring determination of these elements in proper sequence.

My logic and rationale for the system was this. The communications function must be managed. The flow of relevant information downward, upward and laterally must be planned, organized, coordinated, measured, and monitored. It must have a defined vision—the ideal state of communications; mission—the purpose and role of the communication staff; philosophy—principles and tone of employee communications conduct.

Furthermore, the system must:

- Enhance the current communications process by strengthening the focus on achievement of business objectives.
- Translate the business plan, both strategic and tactical, into terms that employees at every level can understand and support.
- Identify key audiences/levels/groups within the organization.
- Address current employee beliefs and expectations. Create collaborative interface among all employees.
- Increase trust between management and the workforce.
- Provide measurements of progress towards employee commitment and goal achievement.
- Facilitate determination of what is relevant information.
- Encourage shared knowledge learned from training.
- Coordinate management speaking with one voice.

The plan is the package of documentation that describes everything from the vision to the desired outcome of each issue to the timeline for implementation to the goals. It must define the issues and the key audiences in addition to naming the channels to be used.

Organizing resources around the plan requires that the people involved understand how downward, upward and lateral information sharing should work and their role in it, equipment is available for meetings, video playback and budgets are established for the activities.

Coordination requires the assignment of communications staff to specific duties for oversight, implementation and facilitation of communications actions.

Monitoring embodies regular review of the progress of implementation relative to the outcomes called for in the plan and making necessary adjustments.

Since Synchronous Communications is issues-driven, defining the issue is paramount. Then it is a matter of determining the right information, the right audience, the right time and the right channels to create awareness, understanding, acceptance and actionable support. This definition begs the questions:

- Who, what levels or what groups specifically comprise the audience?
- What are audience current beliefs and behaviors toward the issue?
- What is the desired outcome of the information?
- What relevant information must be shared with each audience to achieve that outcome?
- What mix of channels must be used to convey the information to each audience?
- What is the most effective timing, frequency, sequencing or cascading of the message?
- How is the audience moved from their current beliefs and behaviors to desired beliefs and behaviors?

I concluded that the model must contain 11 components: communications issue; target audience; audience current beliefs/perceptions; desired outcome; message/information; timing/frequency; print channel; face-to-face channel; video/audio channel; symbolic channel; measurement.

From this model came a worksheet of 11 components in sequence and an expanded listing of factors for consideration under each of the components dealing with Synchronous Communications. Application of this sequence is depicted in Chapter 7.

- Define Communications Issue
- Identify Specific Audiences for Issue
- Research Each Audiences Current Beliefs/Perceptions Concerning Issue
- Decide Desired Outcomes For Each Audience

- Identify/Develop Information/Messages
- Consider Print Channel
- Consider Face-to-Face Channel
- Consider Video/Audio Channel
- Consider Symbolic Channel
- Set Timing/Frequency of Message
- Establish Measurements of Success

Defining the communications issue is the springboard from which all the other components are decided. The definition could be as brief as "Quality improvement" or as long as "A new quality measurement indicator developed by the organization." For each issue, a separate mini-plan is required.

Target audience is the next consideration. Who ought to know about the issue? A few individuals? A certain department? A specific group of employees including new employees? Various job levels such as middle management, first-line management, hourly employees and salaried employees? Since each job level has different responsibilities, each has different information needs, therefore, a separate plan is required for each audience.

Current beliefs and perceptions of the target audience about the issue may be determined by research or by assumption. Since employees are a captive audience, their knowledge about the issue may be generally known. By listing current beliefs and perceptions, knowledge gaps will become obvious and can be addressed in the process.

Deciding desired outcomes demands a purpose for the communications. Is it to make employees aware? Create understanding? Encourage acceptance of the issue? Move people to actionable support on the job? What should employees do with the information? Share it with other employees? Does it fit with the organizations plan?

Information content and message must be crafted so that there is a constructive transition from current beliefs to the desired outcome. As advocates of relevant information sharing, communications manager's must facilitate objective exchange of factual data. Pro's and con's of the issue may be presented. Persuasive conclusions that are aligned with the organization goals and employees values are acceptable. The information should help the audience think through the issue.

Additional considerations for message development are: determine its tone; tell what and how the issue impacts the audience—what's in it for them; explain why the issue is relevant; stimulate hopes and desires; use emotion; use past and learning's from history; ask questions; appeal to achievement, self-actualization, encouragement of others and being receptive to others; explain their role or how it has changed; state what is expected of them; give four convincing points to solidify formation of beliefs; give the facts; give context and perspective to the issue; appeal to people's dignity and intelligence.

In general, message content must have meaning for employees. Its context must fit with the organizations culture and it must be consistent over time to maintain credibility. Additionally, in the organizational world, repetition of message is almost mandatory and framing, reframing and reframing the issue is also essential. Furthermore, the formal information that comes from management must be based on a continuum so that employees see the connection between the information at this stage and what was said before and later. This is where the knowledge from training that is going on in the organization fits in to keep it alive.

The four most widely used channels to transmit information—print, face-to-face, video/audio and symbolic—may be used separately or in combination with one another. The more complex the message the more the need for the face-to-face channel either one-on-one or in a group.

- Print—newsletter's, brochure's, memo's, letter's, poster's, billboard's, FAX, e-mail, WEB home page.
- Face-to-face—one-on-one discussions, group discussions.
- Video/audio—video tape, closed circuit and satellite TV, radio program for employees, audio cassette's, telephone, voice mail recording's, iPod.
- Symbolic—actions of leadership, who sends message or is quoted, speeches by expert or one in authority, organizational policy, third-parties, celebrities, legendary hero's, event management, ritual, slogans, themes and ceremony.

Meetings are perhaps the most influential form of ritual and event. It suggests to employees that they and the issue are important. Meetings also create opportunities for meaningful interface and significant emotional experience with other employees. Sometimes the event, such as a conference, breakfast, luncheon, dinner or special ceremony or its location, is the message.

Events also reinforce the message, however its staging must resonate with the audience. Incorporating "sensing" (what people see, smell, hear, taste and touch) into events also helps to bolster the message. Psychologists say that sense of smell stirs up some of our deepest emotional memories. Hearing ranks a close second in triggering recollections of the past—particularly from words and melody in music.

Setting the timing, frequency, sequencing, cascading and phasing of the message are as critical as the message itself. Sometimes timing is everything. If it is too early or late the message loses impact. With the proper frequency, reinforcement of the message instills it in the minds of the audience. Sequencing and phasing enable gradual acceptance of the issue and reduces information overload. They also lend themselves to establishing a timetable and calendar for issue communication. Cascading the message from one audience to the next ensures that certain people receive it before others.

Measurements of progress and attainment are perhaps the most complex tasks. It is difficult to quantify communications effectiveness, however, once desired outcomes are determined, it is easier to compare the desired outcome with the current beliefs of the audience. Changes in employee perception relative to improvement in information flow, timeliness of information, being heard, trusting management, being trusted with information and working more collaboratively with others, are meaningful indicators of progress.

To determine the strengths and weaknesses of the communications process, a periodic audit is necessary. The audit should be a regular and thorough study of communication strategy, philosophy, concepts, flow, sources, audiences and practices within the organization. It is not an employee climate survey or readership gauge. It is about the process and relevant information flow. The outcome of an audit is to use the information to enhance communication flow and eliminate deficiencies.

Employee polls about issues are another method to track awareness and support. These may be done on an as-needed basis. The important thing is to keep testing the pulse of the organization in order to stay on top of the organizations knowledge of what is going on. Meaningful communications statistics will help decide where to tweak the process to keep employees effectively focused.

MEASURING INFORMATION FLOW TO, FROM, AMONG EMPLOYEES

I developed a Communications Effectiveness Inventory (CEI) which provides a comprehensive and coherent audit of the three-way flow of information, including the identification of topics of interest to employees and management. The inventory is flexible enough to customize it for various kinds of organizations. Some 60 questions are offered for employee agreement or disagreement. Among them are:

- My organization keeps employees well-informed about its plans, programs, problems and progress.
- Official communications tell the full story.
- When my immediate supervisor gives me information, I believe it.
- When top management gives me information, I believe it.
- Communication between my department and other departments is good.
- I get enough work-related information to perform my job effectively.
- Management is committed to information sharing.
- I usually hear things from the grapevine before I hear them officially.
- I know and understand the vision and mission of my organization.
- I know and understand the goals and objectives of my organization.
- Upper management listens to employee's ideas and suggestions.
- My immediate supervisor listens to my ideas and suggestions.
- Top management does a good job of explaining its decisions.
- Communication about change is timely.
- Communication about change is effective.
- My organization discloses bad news as well as good news.
- Communication has improved in the past year.
- I am empowered to communicate and take productive action with persons outside of my work group.
- I am empowered to communicate and take productive action with persons inside of my work group.
- Other departments share work information with my department.
- My department shares work information with other departments.
- Employees in my department share work information with me.

The inventory also provides for identification of current and preferred sources of information. Usually, the current source of most information is the grapevine while the immediate supervisor is the preferred one. Issues and topics of interest range from how well the organization is doing in the marketplace to where it is going and how it is going to get there; from where employees fit in to the status of the competition and from the future of the company to cost reduction programs and sales outlook.

When CEI indicators of downward and upward communications are high, employees feel empowered and are willing to give discretionary effort on the job. When measures of lateral communications are high, employees are working autonomously and collaboratively because they know what must be done and feel they have been empowered and entrusted with critical information to perform, individually and collaboratively, with little oversight. It is Empowered Autonomy.

Within two years of the establishment of the Automotive Components Group, a strategic communications plan was in place which dealt with every stakeholder of importance to the new unit including employees, trade and general media, government officials and communities in every part of the world where operations were located. And it was aligned with the new strategic plan that was developed for the components group.

While this was going on, I took it upon myself to establish formal communications with the other three groups that GM had created a few years earlier. I contacted the public relations group directors of Buick-Oldsmobile-Cadillac, Chevrolet- Pontiac- Canada and GMC Truck and Bus and asked them to meet on a monthly basis to share information about group activities. They agreed. We rotated monthly meeting locations and I served as chairman of discussions.

This led to several things: a corporate PR director was invited to join the team so that communication was coordinated across GM, the groups picked up on the ACG communications plan and initiated their own, a career path process for all corporate PR staffers was designed and I was appointed to serve on the charter communications team for the new GM-UAW Quality Network that was organized in the mid-1980's.

FROM GM, TO DOW CORNING, TO MY OWN CONSULTING COMPANY

I left GM in June of 1992 and joined Dow Corning Corporation in Midland, Michigan that same month as head of external corporate communications and in charge of reestablishing its good reputation after the breast implant crisis broke on the national scene.

GM had recently appointed the vice president of marketing to also head the Public Relations Staff following the retirement of the PR vice president. Four other senior PR executives and I expected to be considered for the job. We saw that corporate decision as a sign to downgrade the PR function. Three of us left GM not too long thereafter.

My accomplishments at GM in communications and crisis communications—which included the peaceful resolution of an employee taking 14 other employees hostage at gunpoint in a Fisher Body plant in Pontiac, Michigan; the 13-year-old environmental situation at the Fisher Body plant in Lansing, Michigan; the deposing of allegations by the Detroit News that Fisher Body patternmakers had an unusually high rate of death from cancer, and the effective mediation of a new employee hiring dispute at Saginaw Division's Alabama operations between GM and the UAW and between GM and county commissioner's backed by Governor George Wallace—were enough to convince the president of Dow Corning to support my being hired.

Regarding crisis communications, the Synchronous Communications Management system lends itself, very well, to the development of a crisis communications plan and I created one at Dow Corning. By identifying a series of scenarios that the organization could conceivably face, a well thought out response to any situation would be available at a moments notice.

The first thing I did at Dow Corning was to seek out and meet with members of major newspapers to establish a dialogue with them and set straight the company's position on the breast implant controversy. This was a move on my part to break away from a strategy by a retained outside public relations agency's which called for communication through third-parties. More facts about the issue gradually started to appear in those publications.

Next, I started a dialogue with the U.S. Food and Drug Administration to understand its position on the product. No study on breast implants ever proved they caused cancer or auto-immune disease. Yet, the FDA allowed that perception to continue and I was determined to persuade them to acknowledge this evidence and support Dow Corning.

I was on the verge of teaming Dow Corning with wives of members of the National Basketball Association Detroit Pistons to fight breast cancer and dispel the myth that breast implants caused cancer, when the president of the company took an early retirement. His departure drastically changed the complexion of my job and I left.

After leaving Dow Corning and starting my consulting company, I came across a potent diagnostic tool that identified and measured valid and statistically significant factors of organizational culture. This was an exciting discovery to me because I had been trying to enrich the quality culture model I developed at Saginaw Division. I was looking for something that would serve as an indicator of organizational values and norms. This was it and more. I figured that if employee perceptions of organizational behavior could be identified and rated, communications could be used to focus management and employees on constructive performance and steps could be taken to address elimination of unproductive behavior.

Organization's have a personality just like people do. Some are competitive, pushing employees to outperform each other while others encourage them to work together collaboratively. The personality reflects the signals—often subtle and unspoken—that management sends to employees about how they are expected to act. Over time, these signals become patterns that make up the culture and determine the way things are done.

Cultures created intentionally or unintentionally can be positive or negative. In fact, some organization's management are shocked to discover they actually are rewarding behaviors that have a negative force on job performance and the bottom line.

The indicator that I discovered helps profile an organization's culture based on specific behaviors that are expected of the employees. Behavioral expectations are easier to measure and interpret than other aspects of culture and have a more direct impact on the way employees approach their work and interact with one another. These norms encourage employees to strive for high quality results. Others norms work against the attainment of quality.

I now often use this device, in tandem with my Communications Effectiveness Inventory, as an indicator of organizational achievement as noted in the Achievement Culture Index listed in the Addendum. I think it is suffice to say that another book could be written about this component that I call our Applied Culture Management system. There are additional details about it in The Addendum.

7

WORKING THE SYSTEM DAILY

Defining communications issues, incorporating
them into the ongoing process

On the basis of the *Public Relation Journal* description of Synchronous Communications as "a classic system," and other endorsements, the driving force behind its daily implementation is worthy of note and examination.

The most difficult part of inducing change in communications at Saginaw was to continuously convince top management that it will help them succeed. I decided that every increment of doing something different had to be "sold" to them in advance. There should be no surprises because every product or service my staff provided was so visible to so many people and a great deal of communication plan implementation involved manager's and immediate supervisors from other staffs.

This did not mean that other executives were looking over my shoulder micromanaging my department. That was not the case. Building up the function in a relatively short period of time came as a result of a persistent and methodical approach to inform, educate and persuade the executive staff. Their buy-in and commitment were crucial in expanding the role of communications and I wanted to maintain their high confidence in me, my staff and the process.

In times of business downturns, there were occasions when I had to vigorously argue to keep my staff intact. Personnel layoffs were one of the first acts in reducing costs. The traditional method to decrease head-count was based on a percentage of each staff and PR was always the first one to be chosen. My point in resisting was that PR should be regarded as a fixed cost. Unless the layoff was a large one of several thousand employees, it still took the same number of PR staff to manage the process. And, it was in times like this that communication is most urgently needed to keep the remaining employees focused.

It starts with the creation a vision – every employee is aware of, understands, accepts and supports the goals and objectives – and a communications plan that is directed at engaging every level and every individual in sharing information downward, upward and laterally. It then involves orchestrating plan implementation, translating the complexities of the organization's strategic plan into easy-to-understand pieces of information, and ensuring that management speaks with one voice and listens to employees with all ears.

I saw the overall mission of the department being one of liaison between the management/immediate supervisor and the workforce.

Most of the communication issues that arose on a daily basis were my responsibility to identify and handle with my staff. Occasionally, something came along that required consultation with the general manager or executive staff head. And every so often, when I felt that a new approach should be taken on an issue, I discussed the situation with the general manager to make him aware, suggested a course of action and asked him to think about it until I got back to him. The benefits of doing this were to give him a better sense about my thinking patterns and strategy and giving the concept time to incubate in his mind. It compelled him to devote time and thought to communications issues. As a result, he became very receptive and supportive of expansion of the process. He also gained more confidence in my abilities and effectiveness.

Once the daily newsletter, monthly tabloid, mandated meetings, bi-monthly video and other mechanisms were in place, the challenges became the full-scale synchronization of them and meeting management and employee expectations.

The weekly executive staff meeting with the general manager was my major source of relevant information. Much of the information formally shared with others in the division originated at this meeting. Project status, financial data, sales, budget, task team reports and key operational information consumed most of the four-hour session. And part of it included discussion and decision-making.

Before adjournment, the general manager and each staff head shared information they felt was important for the others to know. Usually it involved issues from their respective staffs which generated questions from the other executives. After my report, which I made a point to give at every meeting so that communications' presence was kept visible and tied to strategic discussion, I asked the last question called for on the divisional generic agenda, "Who else needs to know what went on here?" That always provoked useful responses.

The executive staff members would ask the same questions at the end of their departmental meeting and so on down the line.

The weekly meeting with my staff immediately followed the executive staff session. I wanted my group, including my secretary, to learn about those proceedings as soon as possible so that any urgent communication issue could be addressed and acted upon. Each member, including the ones hooked up by telephone conference call at sites outside of Saginaw, was given the opportunity to report on individual activities and query the others. I did the same.

I also tried to give my staff an idea about what I was considering to improve internal or external communications or better implement strategies and how I would approach it. My thinking out-loud was an attempt to demonstrate how my mind worked when it came to communications management so that they could visualize and learn how to effectively manage the system. Their input was solicited, too, and my door was open to them to offer ideas and information.

In recent years, it came to light that my willingness to openly share and inquire produced long lasting affects. Four members of my staff are now directors of communications and public affairs at GM and Delphi. They have kept in touch with me and the others over the years. Occasionally, when they talk with one another about problems they have in common, I have been told that they ask "What would Ron do?" It is satisfying to hear that, but even more gratifying to know that they learned how to go about dealing with issues. The invaluable input they gave me just a few years ago, which strengthened the Synchronous Communications model, confirms that belief.

In every meeting I asked my staff to help me identify emerging issues in the division that our department should be aware of as the eyes and ears of the company. They in turn asked plant editors and people on other staffs to keep them posted. This developed into an outstanding source of intelligence relating to employee—and management—attitudes, behavior and expectations. Sometimes the issue extended across all plants and offices. Other times it was local to one or a few. In all cases the issue was discussed with my staff and a decision was made whether I needed to refer it upward, downward, laterally or have the department take it on as a communication issue concerning a specific audience.

Many times the emerging issue was a rumor or a half-truth. And that told me that we as communications managers had missed something in our quest to wipe out the grapevine and rumor mill. We may never accomplish that, but that was the goal. Communications is an ongoing process that must have continuous oversight and immediate detection and correction of imperfections. It is like trying to build a quality product and being interrupted by defects. So goes it in communications, the difference being that defects are usually caused by lack of relevant information.

I knew that whatever information went into the publications and video had to be a balance between the interests of top management and those of employees. Executives are concerned about the issues that make the difference between profit and loss and success and failure such as product quality, cost reduction, the competition, the organizations future, product development and employee relations. Employees want information that helps them understand their work environment and their relationship to it. They want to hear about the organizations' future, the competition, reasons for organizational actions and decisions, goals and direction, why it is going that direction, how it will get there, employee benefits, product quality and financial results. There is some overlap, but there are some differences.

And that is where the judgment of the communications staff comes into play. It is not a situation whereby employees are told how to think about issues. It is more an emphasis on what to think about and having confidence that employees will respond in a constructive manner. It is trusting and empowering employees with relevant information in order to unite the organization in achievement.

The planning and development of each of the major communications products—newsletter, tabloid, video, meetings—were a collaborative effort at Saginaw. The communications staff person responsible for the finished version and I agreed on the topic and story angle and then that person worked out the details. I would review, edit and give final approval before it was released. I also helped coordinate cross-promotion of the issue so that a major story due in the tabloid or an upcoming video program would receive brief blurbs in the daily newsletter in advance.

Every product of the communications department exceeded expectations. The daily newsletter delivered brief, timely reports about significant happenings in the division, GM or the industry. Future events and plans were announced. It was used to recognize exceptional employee performance, welcome customers and potential customers to the division, publicize new contracts for products, explain management decisions on key issues, identify the competitor companies, describe quality issues and improvements, illustrate tallies on cost reduction and more.

The tabloid, being a monthly, allowed for more in-depth articles on a relaxed schedule. However, the time it took to obtain approval for story accuracy sometimes just met the printing deadline. Stories were written "newspaper-style" and limited to capsule-length. There were few if any stories that were carried over to other pages. Employees, management, union leaders, suppliers and others were interviewed and quoted as best-sources of information.

To keep the big picture of the business in front of employees, a column was run every issue called "The General Managers Corner." The content ranged from an overview of how Saginaw stacked up in the industry and why to how the division got or lost a major contract to explaining management decisions.

Excerpts from some of the columns include:

Realignment strengthens Saginaw, supports customer's needs—As competition in the auto industry continues to increase, we need to establish a stronger relationship with customers and potential customers. Before the new realignment, customers were supported on an overall divisional basis. There was no specific divisional contact person assigned to a particular customer. At times we had to spread our resources too thin and contact with some customers went lacking.

By establishing individual business units by product line, we now have the personnel assigned to work very closely with each customer.

In keeping with this focus on the customer, I am asking every employee to remember that our customers include everyone from the next Saginaw person in line, to the person who installs our products on the vehicle, to the man or woman who buys that vehicle.

Reward the right behavior to get the right results, fail to reward the right behavior and you're likely to get the wrong results.—Those words come from Michael LeBoeuf, a University of New Orleans management professor who wrote an article entitled 'The Greatest Management Principle.'

As part of Saginaw Divisions efforts to become a world class organization, the staff and I have committed to improve our management style and rewards and recognition for employees are an important element of that. But what is the right behavior? It comes in many forms. Quality work is one of them. Creativity, innovation, intelligent risk-taking, decisiveness, working smart, finding and eliminating waste, and simplification are others. We will also recognize people for their trust in Saginaw Division and their spirit of teamwork.

There are already some excellent ways of recognizing and rewarding employees going on in the plants and offices. Whenever I read in the divisional daily *Newsletter* about someone who detects a quality problem, I write them a letter commending them for their action because I am appreciative that they helped avoid making a customer unhappy.

<u>Employees encouraged to learn about the business</u>—Our competitive challenge is to make top quality automotive components at prices that are competitive worldwide. That increases the need for everyone who works at Saginaw Division to understand, not just what Saginaw is trying to accomplish, but how Saginaw expects to go about it and how everyone fits in.

During the past several years, I have seen an increase in employees' sophistication about the business. I have witnessed this change in my scheduled monthly face-to-face meetings with employees, and our own employee communications surveys bear this out: employees are being asked to do more independent thinking and are asking in turn for more information about Saginaw's plans and strategies. We must nurture, rather than stifle, that attitude. And we are doing just that with a network of publications, video programs and face-to-face communications within the division.

There is no doubt that face-to-face meetings are the most important element of the system. It is the one place where information is shared from supervisor to employee, from employee to supervisor and among employees. It doesn't get any better than that.

<u>What world class means to me</u>—What is expected of us when we say we are a world class organization? I like to think it means being better than our competitors.

Earlier this year, I began to have a real concern that in our attempt to become world class, we may lose sight of the fact that winning is far more important than simply matching an opponent. I worried that a feeling may settle over us that said, "The Japanese are so far ahead of us, we might not be able to beat them, so we better concentrate on becoming as good as they are."

But then I realized that playing second fiddle to anyone just isn't our style.

I have always admired the late Vince Lombardi, National Football League head coach, who said, "I've never met a good loser." I also appreciate the comments of John Wooden, the former basketball coach at UCLA, who was asked why he concentrated so hard on winning. His response, " If winning isn't important, then why keep score?"

There is a winning attitude at Saginaw Division that will give us the edge. Our spirit of working together will make us world class in quality, price, delivery and service.

This winning attitude is vitally important because our customers are keeping score.

Employees question jobs for offspring.—During several of my visits to Saginaw Division's plants and offices, one question which has been voiced quite often by employees has been about the supply of future jobs for their children at that location.

I share this concern with you. For many years, Saginaw has employed generations of families. Now, we and other GM operations are facing the toughest competitive challenge ever. The way for us to meet this challenge is to become more productive.

What is productivity? Well, it is a very misunderstood word. But it is not working harder.

Mobil Corporation, in one of its public issues messages, had this to say about it:

"It is the relationship of goods and services produced in the economy compared with the resources used to produce them. Output per labor hour is the measure most widely used. This doesn't necessarily mean the output per hour of a person picking tomatoes . Productivity is a function of the machinery worker's use, and the technology that designs, maintains, and often operates the equipment.

"Productivity means working smarter with better tools. Productivity stems from investment in plant, equipment, research, and people.

"Increased productivity is crucial because it is the only way to raise real incomes, remain competitive and keep inflation in check. Productivity is the key to an expanding economy and a bigger pie that can accommodate the needs of the workers and the poor and disadvantaged."

The goal of the tabloid was to be the official and honest word of management. It presented the issues in as balanced a perspective as possible and in such a way that demonstrated management was sharing information that employees wanted and needed to know. And employees reciprocated by giving discretionary effort and valuable suggestions for improvement.

An innovation of sorts that I conceived for the tabloid involved interviews with persons from "the plant/office floor." Rather than have employees submit questions about company issues, employees were randomly selected from each U.S. site and asked a question. The question of the month selected was tied to something of significance that was going on in the division and worded in such a way that it could not be answered with a "yes" or "no." This forced the employee to respond with an expanded statement. Five responses were published along with a photo of the employee. What this did was get employees to associate company goals and objectives with activities in their area of work and explain how they were or were not being met or applied. It also gave the communications department feedback on whether information sharing was working and at what level.

Some of the questions and responses for the Comments column were:

What improvements have resulted in your department as a result of the synchronous (lean manufacturing) process?

Tom, machine operator, Saginaw, Michigan: "We have contact with vendors now. It also brings employees and management closer together. Employees have more say in their jobs and a better understanding of job requirements and functions. I think the process is working. It's a team effort."

Janice, assembler, Saginaw, Michigan: "The process needs more improvement. Management is not with us 100 percent. Small problems are not taken care of until it results in a larger one. The superintendents don't react quickly enough to line problems."

Antonio, tube presser, Athens, Alabama: "We have seen significant improvement in the reduction of scrap and rework, as well as the reject rate. Our manpower has been utilized better and as a result everyone works much better together."

Margaret, statistical process control operator, Detroit, Michigan: "We have less inventory in our department, which is a good thing. Also, our bottleneck areas show up more clearly. This helps us identify problems more quickly."

What would you do to improve communications?

Carl, production supervisor, Buffalo, New York: "Communications is getting better. Management at this plant is more honest with people. We need to see more action and follow-up. When that doesn't happen, communications becomes a program and turns people off."

Gail, engineer, Saginaw, Michigan: "Face-to-face communications at my job location are very good. There is a closer relationship with engineers and people on the plant floor."

Bryan, press operator, Athens, Alabama: "Use overlap time between shifts to discuss problems and quality."

Delorice, assembler, Detroit, Michigan: "Have more one-on-one meetings. A lot of people are scared to speak up in a group."

What actions are you taking to make your job more secure?

Dennis, production supervisor, Buffalo, New York: "One of the biggest things I try to do is leave no doubt that I'm committed to achieving our quality goals. I check and document parts more often."

Thomas, utility operator, Athens, Alabama: "I do the best job possible keeping our department clean and free of debris. I feel that by taking pride in cleanliness a better working environment is created. People feel better about themselves in a clean and organized area, therefore, productivity and quality are better."

Eileen, spline roller operator, Detroit, Michigan: "I go to the source of the problem. Before, I might have let it go because I felt we could afford to. Now, by going to the source, I help keep bad parts from leaving the plant."

The division has set 6% as the goal to reduce costs. What is your unit doing to reduce costs?

Ralph, purchasing supervisor, Detroit, Michigan: "We have reduced the inventory of raw materials and in-process parts to cut the amount of money tied to those items and increase inventory turns."

Ted, tool inspector, Saginaw, Michigan: "Our Performance Team studied the inner and outer race assembly and developed a method to plot trouble area charts each day. We pinpointed the problem and fixed it so that it will not reoccur."

Wendy, gear roller operator, Buffalo, New York: "We plot and post charts of scrap performance. By doing so, scrap and rework has significantly decreased."

To better plan the content of future issues, a matrix was developed for the tabloid which called for specific types of articles at predetermined frequencies for the subsequent 12 issues of the publication. For example The General Managers

Corner and the Comments column were to appear every month, a story about a quality assurance process was scheduled monthly for 12 months and then for every other month thereafter, status of performance to budget was to appear monthly, cost reduction updates set monthly and so on. A certain amount of space was reserved for recent developments and "breaking news."

Performance to budget is a very important issue at GM. Based on sales forecasts for the new model year, divisions were "allocated" funding to cover all costs. Those dollars are tracked relentlessly by both GM and the division. The thought occurred to me that because this was such a vital issue, employees ought to be aware of its importance, understand how it is managed and learn what actions they can take to help keep it under control.

The first obstacle confronting this initiative was that GM financial reporting consolidates all corporate operations. Saginaw could not divulge its profit or loss numbers independently. After discussing the idea and the situation with the finance director several times, I asked if presenting monthly budget performance numbers as a percentage, over or under allotment, would be acceptable. It was and I then crafted a chart which illustrated that condition to serve as a score card for monthly and year-to-date budget standing. A side-bar story was placed next to the chart to provide explanation of its meaning and point to areas for improvement.

That concept was copied by plant newsletter editors to focus attention on plant budget performance which greatly contributed to the divisional savings realized—from 2.8 percent to 4.9, 3.2, 3.7, 2.2, 5, and 5.5—during the seven-year-period I was there.

Saginaw was always among the top division's in GM's Employee Suggestion Program. The first year of my service there the average suggestion award was $864 per eligible employee. The last year it had increased incrementally to an average of $5,748. To keep the issue in front of employees, a running report on suggestion awards appeared in the *Newsletter*.

As opportunities for quality improvement and cost reduction were publicized and discussed through the various channels of established communications, employees responded in overwhelming numbers and with ingenious recommendations. And as the momentum of communications management and information sharing rose, so did the level of sophistication to promote it.

To preserve employee enthusiasm and sharpen the focus on the business plan, a theme was selected—The Journey to WorldClass—to correlate with the divisions' strategic plan update and revision. The message of the theme was meant to imply to everyone in the division that the effort to become the best in the world would be an ongoing process requiring weekly if not daily gains in the way products and services were designed, manufactured, sold and maintained.

It was in this plan revision that "Enhance Management Style" became a major objective. Divisional leadership had come to the realization that management words and actions were the key to the organizations success and that this factor—leadership—should be become a formal part of the units strategy.

Employees were told in a number of ways that the journey's destination was expected to be a moving target influenced by the world marketplace and the competition. To the extent that Saginaw men and women were aware of the divisions' direction and goals, understood what was required of them, accepted that role and gave full commitment and effort, the journey would be a successful one, one that would ensure job security and company longevity.

The unveiling of the journey began with the Executive Conference which was held at the Grand Hotel, Mackinac Island, Michigan. The general manager and executive staff members each presented a portion of the plan to the other executives in attendance describing the vision, strategy, goals and objectives to be met during the next few years. A question and answer session followed before adjournment and fellowship.

The event included stage-setter films that established the premise of the topic and tone of what was to be presented. A celebrity, Mike Vance, former dean of Disney University, addressed the group at dinner and reinforced the theme of the conference and the plan by discussing innovation. Attendees received a momento, with theme logo, of the event and were requested to display it in their office as a front-runner of employee momentos and merchandise to follow.

The desired outcome of the conference was exceeded. A significant emotional event had taken place which set the bar high for the next conference, which was headlined by former astronaut Allen Shepard who stressed the importance of planning and following it to the letter. It too energized the divisional leadership for the task ahead.

Next, the general manager and executive staff took the presentations to the Middle Management Conference and then to the First-line Supervisor Conference at each domestic location. This was a planned downward communications deployment which cascaded the message to one level at a time in sequence. The Q and A sessions were the big hit. It was the first time ever employees at those levels met with the divisions' top management. Attendees also received a memento with the theme logo.

All these events were publicized in-house, but the subject matter was not shared with hourly and salaried employees until after the sessions for first-line supervisor's were completed. This was conducted by immediate supervisors face-to-face with their work group and in conjunction with the daily newsletter and tabloid publicity. The same sequence of conferences was repeated annually as the plan was updated. Each year past performance was reviewed and goals for the upcoming year were set and explained along with strategies for the transition that would be occurring.

To bolster salaried employee participation in the GM Suggestion Program a pilot was developed for the Journey to World Class effort. Called World Class Ideas, the program got off to a flying start as 374 employee Idea Teams were formed , consisting of approximately 8 employees per team. Another 110 employees served in support roles.

Employee teams met once a week to identify potential cost-saving or revenue-producing ideas. Many teams went beyond that and got together on their own time to compare notes and report on research. Team members were responsible for conducting their own research to document costs and to determine whether the ideas were feasible. Then Ideas Action Committees, comprised of employees from personnel, finance, manufacturing and engineering at each site verified the information and decided whether to approve and implement the idea.

As ideas were approved, team members earned points based on the amount of cost savings and could redeem the points for a variety of merchandise from a special gift catalog.

In just the first three days of the formal start, 157 team suggestions were turned in which far exceeded the number normally submitted in a month under the regular program. Ideas approved for implementation were valued at more that $400,000 in savings. Several ideas were valuable enough to qualify for the maximum team award of $20,000.

World Class Ideas generated millions of dollars in cost-savings for the division which would have not been realized without it. And, it garnered a whole lot of teamwork and commitment among employees for years to come. Another thing it achieved—enhanced lateral communications where employees work together autonomously.

The strategic plan continued to be one of the main sources of information for communications managers. They in turn looked to how operations people were converting that data into tactics. Stories were developed about tactical activities, problems and successes, but confidential and proprietary information were protected.

The *Report to Supervisors,* which was distributed to all immediate supervisors from the general manager on down, was meant to aid the people who are in daily contact with the majority of employees. They are the most trusted, are given information by subordinates and are looked to for information. And since employees feel that face-to-face communications is the best channel of information sharing, the immediate supervisor became the most valuable factor of the process. Therefore, the supervisor needed to be supplied with the most relevant information and tips regarding how to better work and talk with employees. Various outside newsletters and publications were scanned to provide this type of information.

One of the articles in the Report that had a far-reaching impact was about asking effective questions of employees, questions that create ownership and put people on the offensive rather than the defensive. The way supervisors ask a question determines the level of support and trust employees feel.

Effective questions empower people. They point to accomplishments and to what people are doing that is working. They nurture creativity and motivate employees.

Some examples of questions from the *Report* are:

- How do you feel about the project?
- What have you accomplished that you are pleased with?
- What kind of help do you need to accomplish the objective?
- What do we need to do to get us where we want to be?
- I'm trying to get an update. How is it going for you?
- How can we improve this?

Questions like these and other tips were also helpful to the general manager and other executives when they met with employees or toured the facilities.

Dialog, the monthly newsletter for plant and staff editors, contained information about interviewing techniques, how to edit and condense articles, how to obtain information about local operations and acceptable writing style.

Joint Activities was a monthly publication that centered on sharing information about management and labor interaction and contractual issues at the Saginaw, Michigan site.

Information generated from the weekly Joint Activities meetings and annual Joint Leadership Conference revolved around four objectives as stated by the divisional personnel director and international representative of the GM-UAW Department: to educate GM and UAW employees on new contract language pertaining to quality and job security; to review new contractual procedures for improving the competitive position of each plant site; to share ideas and product information; to implement a process of reviewing each sites competitive action plan.

A quarterly newsletter, *Insight*, provided details about governmental issues and the GM political action activity, to executives and managers. It encouraged individual contact and correspondence with elected officials about legislation.

21st Century Supplier, a monthly newsletter, was launched to create a stronger partnership with the many suppliers to the division. It was coupled with events such as supplier conferences to enable more detailed discussion face-to-face about quality improvement and cost containment.

USING THE SYNCHRONOUS COMMUNICATIONS WORKSHEET

Each relevant issue that was included in the divisional strategic plan was submitted to the Synchronous Communications Formula's Worksheet for communications development consideration. However, a major issue emerged outside of the plan pertaining to a new just-in-time/lean manufacturing philosophy. Saginaw Division was selected by GM as the site of a pilot operation to test the concept. Since it was such a dramatic departure from the current manufacturing process at GM, communications was looked to as the best way to prepare employees for the profound changes that were to occur. So we plugged the new issue into the Formula as follow:

Phase One

Communications Issue
The new Lean Manufacturing process

Audience
Executives and middle management

Current Beliefs and Perceptions
- Heard about it in the industry.
- Other manufacturers were evaluating it.
- May be future strategy.
- Suspicious of potential and impact on operations.
- Japanese manufacturers use it.

Desired Outcome

Awareness and basic understanding of the process, inform subordinates face-to face at every level about pilot and that more information will be coming from immediate supervisor and divisional publications, inform unions, belief it will make division more competitive, able to answer subordinates questions.

Messages/Information

- GM pilot of process to be conducted at Saginaw.
- Outline purpose, importance, scope and administration of the project.
- Efficiency results from balancing the flow of material not the capacity of equipment.
- Better quality results because in-process inventory is minimized and defects detected more quickly between operations.
- Raw material inventory is used only for products on order and not to utilize employees time.
- Bottleneck operations must be identified hourly/daily and fully utilized 24/7 if necessary to maintain efficient material flow during regular shifts.
- Material/inventory cost savings result from having just enough raw material/parts on hand.
- Profit results from maximizing throughput of ordered product and minimizing all operating expenses and inventory.
- Training program will be forthcoming.
- Status/progress reports.
- The process will be applied to manufacturing operations and office activities.
- Job security may be strengthened.
- Manager to be named to oversee process.

Print Channel, Timing/Frequency

- Handout with summary of information distributed at meeting.
- Meeting evaluation form for feedback.

Face-to-Face Channel, Timing/Frequency

- Middle Management Meeting, next three months.

Audio/Video Channel

- Telephone conference with outlying sites, next three months.

Symbolic Channel
- Event—meeting on site, questions and answer sessions.
- Hosted by general manager and executive staff.

Measurements
- Meeting evaluation by attendees
- Document question/answer session for identification of concerns and topics of interest about process for future communications.

Phase One

Communications Issue
The new Lean Manufacturing process

Audience
Immediate supervisors except executives and managers.

Current Beliefs and Perceptions
- May have heard about it in the industry.
- Other manufacturers were evaluating it.
- Suspicious of potential and possibility of more work for supervisors.

Desired Outcome
- Awareness and basic understanding of the process, inform subordinates face-to face about pilot, more information will be coming in divisional publications, belief it will make division more competitive, able to answer employee questions.

Messages/Information
- GM pilot of process to be conducted at Saginaw.
- Outline purpose, importance, scope and administration of the project.
- Better quality results because in-process inventory is minimized and defects detected more quickly between operations.
- Costs will decrease, quality will increase.
- Training program will be forthcoming.
- Regular status/progress reports will be forthcoming.
- The process will be applied to manufacturing and office activities.
- Job security will not be affected.
- Japanese manufacturers use it.
- Why competitiveness will increase.

Print Channel, Timing/Frequency
- Report to Supervisors newsletter, next three issues.
- List of anticipated questions with answers.

Face-to-Face Channel, Timing/Frequency
Immediate supervisor prepared to answer questions from subordinates.

Audio/Video Channel, Timing/Frequency
None for this phase, prepare program for quarterly video Perspective.

Symbolic Channel
General manager is source for Report to Supervisors article.

Measurements
Random informal mini-poll to determine receipt of information, reaction.

Phase One

Communications Issue
The new Lean Manufacturing process.

Audience
All other employees.

Current Beliefs and Perceptions
- May be suspicious of the process eliminating jobs.
- Some employees may have heard about lean manufacturing.

Desired Outcome
- Awareness and basic understanding of the process.
- Belief division will be more competitive.
- Belief that jobs will be more secure.

Messages/Information
- GM pilot of process to be conducted at Saginaw.
- Outline purpose, importance, scope and administration of the project.
- Better quality results because in-process inventory is minimized and defects detected more quickly between operations.
- Costs will decrease.
- Training program will be forthcoming.

- Regular status/progress reports.
- The process will be applied to manufacturing and office activities.
- Job security will be increased.
- Japanese manufacturers use it.

Print Channel, Timing/Frequency
- Daily newsletter, after Report to Supervisors, then weekly updates.
- Tabloid, next three months.
- Supplier newsletter, after first article in tabloid.

Face-to-Face Channel, Timing/Frequency
Immediate supervisor prepared to answer questions.

Audio/Video Channel, Timing/Frequency
None for this phase, prepare program for quarterly video Perspective.

Symbolic Channel
General manager is source for article.

Measurements
Random informal mini-poll to determine receipt of information, interview employees for initial reaction to process for quote in tabloid.

Phase Two
The second phase of communications for this issue is a reiteration of the above sequence, but building on the information in Phase One and designed for a different outcome at a later time.

Issues promotion by various channels
The first article in the tabloid following the announcement of the new Lean process appeared on the front page with a headline that read: "Just-in-time process gains momentum at Saginaw; Employee awareness and training increase." Below the headline a boxed-in listing of 12 process concepts provided a clip-out for employee future reference.

Just-in-time process concepts

- 1. Material Flow: Goal is to work with a theoretical batch size of one piece.
- 2. Quality: Goal is to have zero defects.

- 3. Man/Machine Effectiveness: People and machines are better utilized only on scheduled components.
- 4. Quick Setups: The goal is 10 minutes or less.
- 5. Scheduling: Production schedules are developed when parts are ordered. Only those parts scheduled are produced.
- 6. Simultaneous Engineering: Total communication and interface between Manufacturing Engineering, Product Engineering and Manufacturing at the earliest stages of designing a product must occur.
- 7. Preventive Maintenance: Preventive maintenance becomes a permanent part of the process.
- 8. Employee Involvement: If employees are to be effective members of the team, they must become part of setting the goals of the organization.
- 9. Supplier Management: Needs of the organization must be communicated to suppliers. Suppliers must be trained in the process.
- 10. Management by Sight: By walking through a plant, employees should be able to see what state the business is in by the amount of inventory and how the critical resources in the plant are operating.
- 11. Training: Employees in the organization must have first-hand knowledge of the process concepts and be able to apply them in their jobs.
- 12. Communications: Employees must be kept informed of business goals and activities and have the opportunity to provide feedback, suggestions and information to management and fellow employees.

The 12 concepts became the systemic map by which the division would operate on its Journey to World Class. It later became the pattern for General Motors.

Once the process and its concepts were launched, daily advances became the fodder for more information sharing to employees, from employees and among employees.

A major story in the tabloid about the preventive maintenance concept at the Buffalo plant captured the interest of all the other Saginaw Division plants. Before the 12 concepts were established, the plant was a three-shift, six-day operation. Marked by unscheduled tool changes and time-consuming model changeovers, it was characterized by excessive downtime, high tooling costs and frequent quality problems.

Within six-months, an innovative scheduling method that builds preventive maintenance into the system was implemented. Developed by plant employees, it called for two production shifts separated by maintenance periods of three hours long. Employees from all three shifts met in small group meetings, discussed the operation and agreed on the method.

Under this approach, a production team is responsible for running the machines. To support them, a maintenance team loads parts into a storage system and changes tools on the in-line machines. Tool changes not affecting hourly output were done during the production period. Those which restricted hourly output were performed during the maintenance when machines are idle.

In addition, employee teams devised a tool change program which allowed the machines to run at least eight hours with no tool change and quick-change tooling to shorten the length of change time.

The first several months of operation under the new method resulted in output rising by 25 percent and indirect labor efficiency increasing by 20 percent. Tool and scrap costs also decreased significantly.

Tom, a first shift jobsetter, said "Before this program, most problems were covered with 'Band-Aids.' Both management and the trades people are listening to one another more."

"My job is more interesting, too. My responsibilities are different and that keeps me thinking."

Charlie, a second shift jobsetter, stated "Management basically said, 'It's up to you to make it happen.' At first, we said 'There's no way that this will work.' But, then we figured, why not give it a try?

"There's a positive attitude spreading around the plant and it's getting other people involved."

Art, a production supervisor, added, "The system really works because everyone is involved and working as one unit."

"Our meetings have become solid business meetings. When I sit down for a meeting, I'm not the supervisor, I'm a member of the team. I speak my mind like everyone else and listen to what others have to say."

Mike, plant manager, summed it up by saying, "The method helped overcome bottlenecks and triggered a dramatic turnaround of the way we work together."

Other concept stories in the tabloid as implementation expanded included results such as:

- Athens, Alabama Plant 23 increased output by 100 percent, inventory turns by 40 percent, assembly quality by 50 percent, on-time customer shipments improved 70 percent and cost per unit was reduced by 11 percent.
- Saginaw, Michigan Plant 2 cut set-up time by 50 percent and saved $700,000 in direct labor cost by changing from computer numerically controlled equipment to less complicated machines.

- Detroit, Michigan Plant 56 reduced repairs and rework on the assembly line from 40 percent to zero, cut inventory 30 percent, improved quality index from 136 to 142, and decreased warranty claims by 77 percent.

Measurements of communications effectiveness were also conducted during this time:

The monthly tabloid *Steering Columns* was highly rated by employees:

- 92 percent read it and found it easy to read.
- 88 percent rated it as very informative.
- 86 percent believed its content.

Employee opinion's about Saginaw's daily *Newsletter* were also high:

- 95 percent read it and found it easy to read.
- 90 percent said it was very informative.
- 88 percent believed its content.

Perspective, the business economics', bi-monthly video program, provided the stage for downward, upward and lateral communications in one setting. The program received strong reaction from viewers divisionwide. Supervisors showed it to their employees during working hours at the regular monthly meeting and facilitated discussion among attendees. Eighty-five percent of all Saginaw Division employees saw the programs according to the Viewing Completion Statements returned to the Communications Department. Second and third shifts viewing were not as high. Several plants recorded 100 percent viewership.

Employee responses to survey questions about the program yielded the following:

- 83 percent of hourly and 81 percent of salaried employees agreed that the program presented important facts about Saginaw activities of which they were not aware.
- 93 and 95 percent of hourly and salaried employees, respectively, agreed about the importance cost and quality play in maintaining a competitive edge.
- 65 and 72 percent hourly and salaried employees, respectively, saw a change in emphasis from quantity to quality at the division.

- 88 and 86 percent of hourly and salaried employees, respectively, felt their supervisor did a good job of conducting the group meeting.
- 75 percent of all employees felt that the video helps them understand the division's business issues.

Representative comments from employees that gave a strong indication communications was helping to turn the division in the right direction included:

- "Good film. Employees know that competition is increasing, employee involvement has definitely increased. Information such as costs has been shared but not completely."
- " Interest in what we can do here to insure competitiveness, still some disbelief and mistrust from select few."
- " We see the importance of doing the job right the first time in order to have quality parts and at the same time be aware of costs."
- "Management should have been listening to subordinates all the time. Why did it take management so long to get employees involved and communicate."
- "I feel there is a general overall concern that is positive. I believe that when people change their attitudes they will have mutual respect and gain the cooperation it takes to accomplish our goals. These videos and newsletters and meetings are beginning to change attitudes and promote trust."

The Synchronous Communications Management framework, with the assistance of a communications manager, also helped various business units to translate the divisional strategic plan into tactical plans.

The Engine Drive Business Unit was given the challenge to reduce the cost of front-wheel drive axle sets by 20 percent by the next model year to retain its competitive edge and obtain new business. According to the cost reduction coordinator, each area of the business unit was assigned a specific portion of the savings: Operations, which included three manufacturing plants, 41 percent; Engineering and Sales 26 percent; Material Management 18 percent; Personnel and Finance 15 percent.

The business unit director and his staff met with one area of the unit every morning to discuss problems and progress. Frequent updates on the plan were reported in a special weekly newsletter to members of the business unit along with success stories. Employees were given key business and competitor information in a bi-monthly video program which was shown and discussed during the regular monthly meeting by the supervisor. In addition, hourly and salaried employees formed plant process control teams comprised of the supervisor, jobsetter, quality inspector, engineer, and production worker and met weekly to examine specific cost reduction ideas.

In the first six months, half of the 20 percent cost reduction was attained with the balance being met three months later. The rest was realized before the yearend.

TRACKING TRENDS, BOOKS AND OTHER TIPS

To track communications and fine tune it on a daily basis, I maintained a high awareness about trends in communications and about human behavior itself. Mike Vance claimed that he read a book a day, so I increased my intake from books about leadership, culture and organizational behavior, although not one a day.

Another tip I picked up from Edward Bernays was to hire college students to abstract a book of interest. Although *Executive Summaries* were available, and I purchased them too, the service did not always have a condensation of the one I wanted.

As a member of the American Management Association, I regularly received a copy of its *Organizational Dynamics*. It contained invaluable information on a variety of topics including culture and leadership. The *Public Relations Journal* was also a must read.

The one publication I read everyday, and still do, is *USA Today*. In fact, we patterned the Saginaw tabloid similar to its format. Its four major sections—national/international, business, sports and lifestyle—are concise and report on information useful to anyone. The use of graphics is also very effective.

And ever since my high school English teacher mandated the *Readers Digest* as part of classwork, I have continued to renew my subscription. It contains a wealth of information on every topic imaginable from current events to call for action and health, and from human drama and tragedy to politics and money. When I entered PR, I used the *Digest* as a pattern to develop a writing style for various kinds of articles.

Whenever an article interests me, I study the content, context, story angle and flow. The exceptional ones are cut out, if practical, and filed.

Because the 11-point sequence of the Synchronous Communications Worksheet is so effective and important, two more examples are offered as tips for the strategic thinking required:

Communications Issue Number 1
The organization's strategic plan

Audience
All levels of management—top, middle, first-line

Current Beliefs and Behaviors
- Top knows there is a plan but thinks it is not comprehensive enough
- Middle heard there is a plan but does not know its components
- Great majority of first-line do not know about such a plan

Desired Beliefs and Behaviors
All levels are aware of the plan, understand it and their role in achieving it and give actionable support to meet its goals

Messages/Information
- The organization's vision statement
- The leadership's mission statement (role) to achieve the vision
- Middle and first-line management must develop tactical mission statements for their respective levels
- The organization's Critical Success Factors to achieve the vision
- Action Strategies to address each Critical Success Factors

Timing/Frequency
Present to all levels before the end of the first quarter

Print Channel
- Memo to all levels announcing dates and details of presentation
- Handout describing strategic plan framework for each member of management
- Overhead transparencies of plan details for presentation

Face-to-Face Channel
Top managers will present plan, in person, to other levels

Audio/Video Channel
- Present organization's promotional video to set stage for the plan
- Tape record and video tape proceedings of the presentation for later use and for use by members who are unable to attend

Symbolic Channel
- Conduct the presentations off-site and provide lunch
- The president calls the meeting to order, welcomes the group and sets the stage for the meeting purpose
- Select top management members present details of the plan
- The president summarizes the meeting, explains what the next steps will be regarding the plan, including development of tactical mission statements, and challenges the members to commit to work the plan
- The president and all members of top management serve on a panel after the presentations to answer questions from attendees. 3x5 cards are provided to attendees to write and submit questions
- Attendees are each presented with a memento of the occasion

Measurements/Goals
- Complete presentations before the end of the first quarter
- 100% attendance at meeting/view video tape or listen to audio tape of the proceedings
- 100% receipt of the handout
- Document attendance/tape review and receipt of handout

Communications Issue Number 2
Current culture norms and values as defined by middle management completing the Organizational Culture Inventory

Audience
Top management

Current Beliefs and Behaviors (of Middle Management)
- Low Achievement—36
- Low Self-Actualizing—34
- Low Encouraging—35
- Low Affiliative—37

- High Conventional—33
- High Avoidance—25
- High Power—31

Desired Beliefs and Behaviors
- Scores for the four Constructive Styles in the mid 40's (Max—50)
- Scores for the eight Defensive Styles below 20

Messages/Information
- Top management will be informed of culture findings and will develop a Leadership Style Statement and personal improvement plans for themselves to maximize leadership style and constructive culture
- A Culture Philosophy Statement will be developed by middle management defining preferred constructive behaviors
- The entire organization will be made aware of these activities to demonstrate that higher management wants to improve their behavior as leaders

Timing/Frequency
- Discuss at next monthly meeting with middle management
- Discuss at annual performance review of top management by president and at annual top management conference

Print Channel
- A report for top management which illustrates findings from the Organizational Culture Inventory completed by middle management
- A Leadership Style Statement developed by top management and middle management
- Self development plans determined by top/middle management
- A Culture Philosophy Statement developed by middle management

Face-to-Face Channel
Discuss at key scheduled meetings per the Meetings Calendar

Audio/Video Channel
Not applicable

Symbolic Channel
- Top management's interest in culture improvement

- The act of conducting the Culture Inventory and follow through
- Key meetings as listed in the Meetings Calendar
- Development of Leadership Style and Culture Philosophy Statements by top management and middle management respectively set policy and commitment

Measurements/Goals
- Inform top management of findings by February 1
- Complete Culture Philosophy Statement by March 1
- Complete the Leadership Style Statement by April 1
- Complete top management self development by May1

8

EPILOGUE

Restating, reinforcing the messages;
urging organizations, universities to adopt

Employee communications is still a relatively young organizational function. When I entered the General Motors Public Relations Staff in 1973, even GM had no such position. It approved a plan to initiate one in 1975 and officially set the program in motion when a chairman's' letter was sent to all officers, executives and staff heads in 1977.

Some other large corporations may have preceded GM in creating that capacity, however, they basically produced a publication. Even public relations was not well understood at that time in the organizational world and still isn't in many cases.

When I was offered a PR job in GM, I asked if I could have a couple of weeks to check out what PR was all about. At that time, PR was associated with publicity, dealing with the news media and community relations. In fact, a magazine article given to me by my predecessor described the PR coat-of - arms as having a martini glass (representing the three martini lunch with reporters), and a typewriter (representing the instrument used for publicity news releases) along with the slogan "Last to know. First to go." To this day, I have found that too many people in management view PR from that perspective.

As I educated myself about PR, I learned that it was essentially a job involving communications. I came to think that PR should stand for People Relations, Proactive Relations and Persuasive Relations. As a student of leadership, I saw a parallel with PR in that they both seek to influence the action of others. And I concluded that internal PR—public relations with a structure—could be the top strategic organizational tool of the future.

Edward Bernays commended me for that way of thinking when I presented my Synchronous approach at his seminar in 1984. He was intrigued by the concept of the internal public and the formulation of the thinking process to reach that audience. He had given attendees the option of proposing a case study as a workshop project. I was the only one to do so. It was about focusing employees on quality.

He came over to the table where I was working on the project with a few other attendees assigned to my team, leaned over to the person sitting next to me and said in his deliberate delivery "Do you know that you are sitting next to a very smart man?" I looked up at him and smiled. I knew, then, that I was on to something of importance.

That feeling was corroborated when I presented the Synchronous format at the 1988 annual conference of the International Association of Business Communicators in Anaheim, California. More than 700 members attended my break-out session. The interest in the audio/visual presentation was overwhelming to me. There were so many questions at the Q and A that the moderator had to interrupt to adjourn the audience for the next session. Hundreds of members left behind their business cards requesting a copy of my presentation. Dozens of requests for a copy were sent to my office.

The evaluations of my presentation were another pleasant surprise. Speakers were rated on a scale of 1-5 with 5 considered excellent. Wendy Goodman, IABC Manager of Conferences, stated in her letter to me about the results "Your overall score was 4.3 well above average and quite an accomplishment given the fact that IABCer's are extremely tough critics."

Many people in the audience mentioned that the Synchronous format was exactly what they needed for their organization. They said there is nothing in the profession like it that standardizes the communication process and nothing that describes how to manage—plan, organize, direct and control—it.

I kept in touch with Bernays about my work by phone and letter. I called him to discuss the Synchronous Communications model that I was putting together when I was promoted to GM's Automotive Components Group. That conversation reminded me of his eight-step process in dealing with an issue. It gave me the idea to design an 11-point format for the Synchronous Communications Formula to make it easier for managers to effectively think through how to get the right message to the right audience at the right time through the right channels.

Bernays was so certain of the power and effectiveness of public relations, as he practiced it, that he undertook a major effort to license the activity in every state. He said that would keep out the "dumbell, quack, knownothing, nitwit, antisocial-in-behavior or crook" who calls himself a public relations counselor. To ensure ethics within the industry, he maintained that PR people should be tested and required to take their own sort of Hippocratic oath and receive legal sanctions for misbehavior.

According to a U.S. Bureau of the Census report at the time, more than 100,000 people say they are in the specialized business of public relations, he said, while the Public Relations Society of America has 15,000 members. He made his point.

He said that the practice of public relations, if practiced correctly, will become an increasingly important element of "every successful adjustment of an idea, a company or an organization with the public because more people are recognizing that their whole life's work depends on information and the public's understanding of it."

Bernays outlined three distinct segments in the development of public relations: the late 1870's to 1900, the "public be damned" period; the early 1900's, Ivy Lee's (another PR pioneer) the "public be informed" period; and, post-World War I, his own "public be followed" period.

I wonder what his fourth segment would be—"public be understood?"

And, I wonder what he would say about organization's internal public and their public relations/communications practitioners?

If my presumption is correct that organizational communications is still in its infancy, then perhaps Ivy Lee's "public be informed" is appropriate. Maybe both—"public be understood and informed"—would be apropos.

As far as the internal practitioners are concerned, I do not think Bernays would speak too kindly of them. Especially in view of the rather mediocre ratings employees give to their organization's communications.

Communication management continues to be an enormously undermanned and underutilized resource in most organizations today. And institutions of higher learning are not contributing enough to help fill that gap by preparing graduates in this area of expertise. Granted, there are many organizations doing an adequate job of dealing with information about select and individual issues, but the depth and breadth of their internal communication system are narrow indeed when compared with what American employees expect at work and what actually occurs.

The conventional practice of organizational communications appears to be one of informing—one way—rather than generating dialogue which is two ways. Lateral communication is an unheard of and unthought of consideration for information flow and yet this is what goes on among employees as work is being performed—for better or worse.

Furthermore, when organizations do inform, they send essentially the same message to all employees even though people at different levels of the organization have different information needs because their role is different. And the dialogue is wanting.

If 2006 is still part of the Information Age and the Knowledge Worker, organizations do not seem to be aware of it. Study after study and survey after survey indicate that a substantial number of employees does not think the organization is doing a good job of information sharing. Too many employee responses, regarding a category or question pertaining to communication effectiveness on the job, come back as a negative.

And the perception gap on communications issues between management and employees, as noted in the Randstad review, is alarming. With a captive audience at hand, management is not doing enough fast enough. Members of the nation's workforce are still not being reached on matters important to their careers and livelihood. SCM is sort of a broadband communications technology that will contribute to resolving the issue.

Although some of people's deeply held beliefs may conflict with organizational values, it is not like dealing with emotional issues entangled with religion or politics. Communication inside the unit is non-threatening. I have found absolutely no one—in any organization—against improving communications. It is like motherhood and quality: every one is for it. So, when management turns on the spigot of relevant information, people drink it up, digest it and usually respond in a responsible manner. Employees must be empowered with information before they can be expected to attain optimum performance.

WHAT OTHERS HAVE SAID

Thomas Jefferson said that only people who are "well-informed can be trusted with their own government" and that everything happens with the consent of the people. May I suggest that only employees who are well-informed will feel trusted by their own organization and will make everything right happen.

Thomas Friedman was quoted in The New York Times as saying "Tap into people's dignity, and they will do anything for you. Ignore it, and they won't lift a finger."

Employees know more about the community and the world around them than they do about where they work. In life away from their vocation, they are parents, volunteers, neighbors, citizens and community leaders who watch television, read newspapers and magazines and listen to the radio to keep abreast—minute by minute, hour by hour—of what is happening in every part of the planet. At their place of employment, it is a different story.

Where do they get information? An occasional monthly newsletter? A bulletin board notice? Their supervisor? An infrequent meeting?

When they do get information is it timely? Does it tell the full story? Is it relevant to their job? The organization? Their expectations? Their interests?

Does the information make them aware of events and management actions before they happen?

Does it help them understand the organization goals? Problems? Customers? Their role?

Is the information believable? Do they accept it as the truth? Do they trust management?

Are employees willing to take action, without being told, to serve the customer? To help the organization succeed? To share relevant information and work with fellow employees to achieve organizational goals? To get the job done right and on time?

Are employees being heard by management? By supervisors? Do they make suggestions? What is their preferred source of information? What is the dominant current source of information?

A *Harvard Business Review* article suggests that no organization will change any faster than it can reach the hearts and minds of its people.

Mihaly Csikszentmihalyi, who taught psychology at the University of Chicago and wrote a book *Flow: The Psychology of Optimal Experience*, joined the Peter F. Drucker Graduate School of Management at Claremont (Calif.) Graduate University in 1999 to teach MBA students about the psychological basis for happiness and fulfillment in business.

He said that leaders of organizations can encourage this state of mind in employees by giving them clear goals, regular feedback, focus on the moment, meaning to what they and the organization do, personal control (empowerment) and a realization that they are completely enmeshed in networks of relationships (communications) with other human beings.

"Personal growth is contingent on the balance of opportunities for action and the capacity to act that a person encounters at work," he said.

"A feeling of connection is one of the fundamental needs of life," says David Niven, associate professor of political science at Florida Atlantic University and author of *100 Simple Secrets of Happy People.*

He says that to experience thoughtful contact (as in communications) with others is a way to see that fundamental human connection in action.

In his book *Leadership,* James MacGregor Burns says that effective leaders act, inspire and persuade others to act for certain goals that represent the values, wants, needs, aspirations and expectations of themselves and the people they represent.

Donald T. Phillips, author of *The Founding Fathers On Leadership* states that leaders must first listen, establish trust, discuss, debate, understand and learn. Effective communications becomes critical because it is the only way to inspire and persuade others.

I will remind management that effective organizational communication is a three-way process and that the Synchronous Communications Management system is an instrument to shape change. Knowledge is a force. Receiving relevant information is empowering to employees and generates trust in the sender. Giving information and being heard validates an employees existence and sense of worth. This will lead to more effective lateral information sharing among employees which creates a higher degree of collaboration, creation and achievement.

With the advent of e-mail, internal communications has taken a quantum leap forward. But, only in limited areas. Management can send information instantaneously to employees who have computers. Employees with computers can communicate with one another downward, upward, laterally and multilaterally. However, the system is subject to information overload and the interpersonal qualities of communications are diminished.

E-mail is not the panacea for communications effectiveness any more than is an organizational newsletter or occasional meeting. The remedy for an organizations information sharing woes is a comprehensive and coherent system, based on applied communication and management technologies, which uses a measured mix of channels, addresses the information needs of management and the workforce and facilitates its flow to, from, and among them.

In my experience, the answer is Synchronous Communications Management—a proactive approach to an interactive process of planning, organizing, coordinating, measuring, and monitoring the flow of relevant information downward, upward and laterally which gets the right information to the right audience at the right time by the right channels and creates awareness, understanding, acceptance and actionable support as a result of continuous follow-through and regular feedback.

Synchronous Communications Management is a system that is based on a body of knowledge—a science—in a simple format that enables effective management of the flow of relevant information throughout the organization. It is a system that is issues-driven and results-oriented. It helps communication managers to identify key internal audiences and their current beliefs. Then it helps them decide how to craft, coordinate and deliver relevant information through a variety of sources, including through various members of management and supervision. It also helps management to listen more effectively. And all this creates shared meaning.

The modus operandi of communications managers must be one of advocate and liaison for information sharing and one of continuous overseer of the system and its plan. They must digest organizational plans and find ways to break them down into understandable tid-bits for dissemination.

In some cases the professional communicator is responsible for direct implementation of strategies to help management speak with one consistent voice. In other situations, coordination and facilitation of information sharing among management, immediate supervisors and employees are their primary tasks. Whatever the case, managers should create opportunities for dialogue among employees and look to perpetuating the flow of information.

Let there be no doubt that the actionable support of employees will be obtained only by the daily working of the plan so that every member of management and the workforce truly receives and sends the right information at the right time by the right channels.

Every meeting that is held must seen as an opportunity to share relevant information about its outcome with someone or some group of employees. Harnessing this dynamic will take some doing because it is so foreign to the organizational mind-set.

Frequent, timely and relevant information sharing will instill not only a new sense of trust, it will create a feeling of "now" and "urgency" to organizational operations at all levels. It will give everyone involved the sensation of real-time empowerment. And like the national news media delivers information to the public on a wide-ranging timeline, from 24/7 on down, the internal communications system must keep organizational issues and activities in front of employees repeatedly through a multiplicity of channels. In doing so, employees will be constantly focused on what to think about, day-in and day-out.

Synchronous Communications Management provides the blueprint to build a comprehensive system of information sharing which focuses and sustains achievement by every employee, from the top to the bottom of the organization.

A constructive and productive culture will emanate as a result of empowering employees with information—a culture that is achievement-oriented and based on receptive, supportive and self-actualizing men and women.

Movie actor Jack Nicholson said "We learn how to kiss or to drink, talk to our buddies—all the things that you can't really teach in social studies or history—we all learn them at the movies."

The flip-side of that for managers may be: We learn how to manage—plan, organize, direct and control—all the things managers need to know are taught in college and at work. But, where do we go to learn about communications management?

The same could be said about other employees. When you think about it, it makes sense that unless we educate people how to be effective at work, the organization won't be successful. Training involves time and some practice. Education requires only sharing information—a transfer of knowledge—that comes through communication. Action is up to the judgment and discretion of the individual. The choices people make at work or at home are driven by the information they receive and how they think about the issues. If an organization really hires people for their hands and minds, then relevant information sharing is imperative.

A recent edition of the Readers Digest had a banner running through its name on the table of contents page that states "Stories about life, advice about living."

Applying that thought to organizations, perhaps some by-words for internal communications could be "Tales about work, information about working."

Director of the Project for Excellence in Journalism, Tom Rosenstiel, had this to say about the study: "Journalism is how people learn about the world beyond their direct experience. It has consequences for what we know, how we are connected and our ability to solve problems."

I think that statement applies to communications at work, too. Work might be just a four-letter platitude to some people. And like two other four-letter words, gain or loss, what ultimately matters or makes a difference is whether or not you talk about them. And if so, what you say about them. And if you listen. Synchronous Communications Management is the system that will help people learn, connect and solve problems. Not only will the organization survive, it will thrive.

Internal communication has been developing for the past 30 years or so with substantial progress made, but in a fragmented, inconsistent fashion. There must be a more concentrated effort to reach niche audiences and critical mass inside the organization as well as home-in on individual employees to develop a deeper bond with them and among them.

There is sufficient empirical evidence to support the point that great numbers of employees are not on the organizational bandwagon. Their beliefs, which influence the way they behave, vary significantly on many communications issues. There are few categories where employees are overwhelmingly positive or give high ratings to their organization's communication with them.

Taking into account the average percentage of nine elements (63%) of the Randstad study and the average of the 16 points in the FranklinCovey assessment (38%), only 50 percent of employee responses were positive.

This correlates with FranklinCovey's "Collective Focus and Execution" score—51 out of 100—that employees gave to their organizations. It is also close to findings of Actis Consulting and other surveys I have examined.

What this means is that, on average, at least 50 percent of the workforce is not contributing discretionary effort. They do enough to get by. The opportunity is here to bring that group onboard and spike organizational performance. Think about the potential for performance improvement just by more effectively communicating with employees. Think about what productivity could be unleashed in a global or domestic economy.

In the seven years I devoted to Saginaw communications, employee commitment and trust went from 44 percent to an organizational revolution in teamwork of 85 percent. The improvement, though impressive, did not come from the total workforce.

My analysis of this result? It took approximately four of those years to establish the communications infrastructure and obtain gains of large proportions. The last two years of my tenure were spent zeroing in on the 15 percent of employees not yet in the fold which yielded smaller incremental increases in performance. We evidently were not getting the right information to them at the right time or through the right channels.

In my estimation, another two years at that division would have seen employee commitment and trust numbers up into the 90 percentile. I do not see any reason why employee support cannot hit very close to the 100 percent mark.

Through more diligent research, the remaining few non-believers can be targeted and won-over with relevant information. Second and third shift employees are prime audiences with special information needs and new employees must be considered as a special stakeholder and dealt with separately. After all, the organization does have a captive audience.

For every organizational issue, there now is a process which will help determine how best to share relevant information with the right audiences whether it originates from management to employees, from employees to management or among fellow employees as they perform their duties on the job.

The Synchronous Communications Management system offers a comprehensive framework, in a formula format, which guides managers in strategically thinking through every issue from a communications standpoint, creating a plan and overseeing it to successful completion. However, that will not happen unless management takes the initiative to incorporate communications management as a top organizational function, devotes the necessary resources to it and adopts this approach. Show me an organization whose manager's have a passion for doing this and I will show you one that consistently achieves.

This knowledge will not be perpetuated, however, without help from institutions of higher learning. They must prepare graduates to take their place in organizations as agent's of change who know how to reach the hearts and minds and spirits of the people so that they will collaborate, create and achieve.

In looking back to what I stated at the outset, it should be apparent and clear that a communications system to focus and sustain a culture of achievement is, without question, an organizations' last functional challenge. Marketing, engineering, manufacturing and finance have been honed to the cutting-edge of their respective technology. However, the effectiveness of communications sorely lags.

Organization's have learned to plan their activities pretty well, but translating that plan into action through the efforts of employees and sustaining it is not happening the way the leadership desires. It might be said that the plan is not worth the paper on which it is written unless it is translated into action. Study after study, year after year highlight this deficiency.

In every situation that Synchronous Communications Management has been applied, even while under development, it has enabled the organization to successfully attain predetermined goals and objectives. The bottom-line, whatever it may be as defined by the leadership, was met and in many cases exceeded.

A most notable result was at Saginaw Division where I was able to establish a firm base and fine-tune it over a period of several years. Trust between management and employees at every level sky-rocketed and productivity snowballed. Another took place at the food service for a large school district. It was recognized internationally as the best among hundreds and a model operation because it met or exceed every criteria for that industry.

THINGS LEARNED FROM WORK AND COMMUNITY

The evolution of SCM is also noteworthy. Starting with my experiences from some two dozen jobs as a high school and college student, then as a manufacturing supervisor, general supervisor, labor relations representative and public relations supervisor at GM's Delco Remy Division, my interest in communications as information sharing grew into a passion. I wanted to find out everything I could about the organization and the job and I wanted others to have that same knowledge.

Further experiences at Fisher Body Division opened new avenues to me. Newsletters, meetings and face-to-face discussions with various stakeholders became tools for success. They helped to generate discussion—dialogue—and nurtured information sharing which led to resolution of issues.

I also received an education about people and community dynamics as a result of civic involvement. I led or served in just about every type of organization imaginable—Boy Scouts, Red Cross, YMCA, chamber of commerce, historical preservation, Junior Achievement, United Way, United Negro College Fund, Urban League, SER, NAACP, Opportunities Industrialization Centers, PTA and more. I observed the behaviors and values of people from all walks of life. I watched how they dealt with and communicated with one another outside of work.

Wherever I worked became the training ground and the employees and management became my research subjects. Whatever I could find to learn about communications became part of my manual. My files today contain materials from publications and seminars dating back to the 1960's. Every step along the way, I came to definitive truths about effectively managing communications flow. These same truths are the ones that are built into the system.

My promotion to Saginaw Division gave me the opportunity to develop a manageable format for the system and triggered these concepts. With a talented staff that expanded from three to a total of 12 and a divisional executive team that came to realize the potential for a well-managed communications process, SCM became a highly valued function.

Working the system daily, then became the critical task of getting the right message to the right audience at the right time through the right channel for each issue.

The right messages of relevant information were drawn from the divisional strategic plan, from success stories on quality and cost reduction in the plants and offices, from problems and issues that arose in the course of everyday activities, from the reporters, from the communications staff, from management, from the general employee, from new customers, from suppliers and from the various meetings that were taking place. Messages were framed, reframed and reframed to present the issue from all angles on a continuum.

The majority of the right audiences are the five levels of employees—executives, middle-management, first-line supervisors, hourly and salaried. Others included plant and departmental newsletter editors and reporters, union leaders and suppliers .

The right times included daily, monthly, bimonthly, annually and at specific times, phases and frequencies.

The right channels were a consciously determined mix of print, face-to-face, audio and video, and symbolism as demanded by the complexity of the message. The meeting, however, is the event that will carry the day. All the channels may be brought into play at a meeting and participants will personally experience them in dialogue with one another.

When I was named to head communications and public affairs of GM's Automotive Components Group (now Delphi), the job of consolidating 15 GM division's communications staffs forced me to transform the SCM format into a system model with a very specific structure. This eased and accelerated the adoption of the process to one that was common to all 15 divisions. It also helped to set the stage for what was to come—competitive analysis of the entire product line—and prepare employees at every level for the changes that would be inevitable.

PRINCIPLES, PLANNING, CONCLUDING

The SCM system is a relatively simple one. It is also scientific, structured, strategic, systematic, systemic, standardized, sequential, specific, synchronized and as some have suggested—seminal. As with any effective process, it has a set of guiding principles. The principles follow.

Principles of Synchronous Communications Management

1. Top management must recognize communications as one of its key functions—plan, organize, direct, control—and communicate.
2. Communicator's must recognize management—plan, organize, direct and control—as part of their function. And that responsibility must be assigned to a member of the top management group at every key, tactical location.
3. Relevant information sharing must be everyone's responsibility, but management must proactively lead it.
4. The flow of relevant information to, from and among employees must be synchronous—the right information to the right employees at the right time by the right channels.
5. Current beliefs and behaviors of employees at every level must be understood by management before those employees are expected to make the transition to desired beliefs and behaviors.
6. Communications must be driven by strategic plans and be issues-oriented.
7. Downward communications must flow from top management to middle management to first line management to other employees or simultaneously from the top level to the others.
8. Upward communications—from subordinate to supervisor, from supervisor to manager, from manager to executive, etc.—must be encouraged by a management group that is receptive and responsive to it which in turn creates dialogue and empowers employees and increases trust.
9. Lateral communications must be promoted and related to employees working collaboratively and autonomously with persons at all levels to achieve organizational goals.
10. Communications must be measured for effectiveness on a regular, consistent and timely basis, monitored monthly by top management and fine-tuned weekly, if not daily, by communications managers for successful outcome.

Expanding on the Principles of Synchronous Communications Management, I will comment on each one.

- **Top management must recognize communication as one of its key functions—plan, organize, direct, control—and communicate.**

There are those who say that management <u>is</u> communications. When you think about that statement, it makes sense. Management gets things done through the efforts of others. They have meetings to discuss issues and create plans. They send memos and letters with directives. They follow-up by phone or in person on progress and problems. They tour operations and talk to employees to see and hear things first-hand, and so on. Therefore, communications must be part of management's defined function. It hasn't been, until now.

- **Communicators must recognize management—plan, organize, direct, control—as part of their function. And that responsibility must be assigned to a member of the top management group at every key, tactical location.**

  Just as managers must add communications to the definition of their function, the reverse is required of communicators. They must add plan, organize, direct and control to the definition of their function. And it follows that since there is a top manager at every key, tactical location there must be a person at that location who is assigned the responsibility of communications management.

- **Relevant information sharing must be everyone's responsibility, but management must proactively lead it.**

  Communications—relevant information sharing—must be part of every job description. That duty must be encouraged and promoted by management. And "relevant" must be defined in every organization according to what is in its strategic plan.

- **The flow of relevant information to, from and among employees must be synchronous—the right information to the right employees at the right time by the right channels.**

  The basics of communications deal with audience, message, timeliness and channels. For every issue and each audience, the mantra must be repeated and followed. And please note that the word "employees" includes management.

- **Current beliefs and behaviors of employees at every level must be understood by management before these employees are expected to make the transition to desired beliefs and behaviors.**

  Unless management understands the extent of employees knowledge about various relevant issues and topics, the right information cannot be shared with them. And because the role of each level of the organization is different, each level has different information needs. Information leads to knowledge and knowledge is power, therefore the right information will empower employees. Here too, the word "employees" includes management.

- **Communications must be driven by the strategic plan and be issues-oriented.**

    The strategic plan represents the very best discussions and decisions of the organization. It is the master roadmap of where the organization wants to go and how it will get there. It won't get there unless that information is shared with the right employees at the right time through the right channels. Ninety percent of information sharing must come from the strategic plan and issues surrounding it. The other ten percent will come from emerging issues that arise. For every key issue, a mini-communications plan must be developed for each audience.

- **Downward communications must flow from top management to middle management to first-line management to other employees or simultaneously from the top level to the others.**

    First-line managers are the closest to the general employee and have a bond with them that top and middle managers lack. First-line managers are looked to by their subordinates for answers and information. They should be not circumvented. They must be kept fully informed through the chain of command.

- **Upward communications—from subordinate to supervisor, from supervisor to manager, from manager to executive, etc.—must be encouraged by a management group that is receptive and responsive to it which in turn creates dialogue and empowers employees and increases trust.**

    Upward communication in the form of questions, complaints, suggestions and information sharing is difficult to generate if the supervisor is not willing to listen and act upon it if needed. A culture conducive to dialogue must be encouraged and nurtured.

- **Lateral communications must be promoted and related to employees working collaboratively and autonomously with persons at all levels to achieve organizational goals.**

    Lateral communications is rarely, if ever, thought about as a formal part of the information sharing process. However this is where the real work and achievement occur. Management must promote this concept so that everyone in the organization knows that they really are empowered to act unilaterally or in concert with others to achieve the right result.

- **Communications must be measured for effectiveness on a regular, consistent and timely basis, monitored monthly by top management and**

fine-tuned weekly, if not daily, by communications managers for successful outcome.

There is a saying that "What gets measured gets done." I add to that statement "and becomes institutionalized." Plus, management understands numbers. If communication's performance is quantified, top management will stay engaged. A monthly review of communications by top management keeps the process foremost in their minds almost as much as financial performance.

The recipe for Synchronous Communications <u>Management</u> involves the following:

1. Plan
   • Define the vision—the ideal state of communications.
   • Determine details of the 11 points to get the right information to the right audience at the right time through the right channels for each issue pertinent to the units strategic direction.
   • Set goals for desired results on every key issue.
   • Document everything that is to be done.

2. Organize
   • Organize human, financial and physical resources.
   • Decide the mission of the communications managers—their role in attaining the vision.
   • Determine the communications philosophy—the role and tone of management, supervision and employees in the communications process.
   • Establish an imbedded reporter network as a news source and as a grapevine and emerging issue monitor.
   • Develop a meetings calendar—a listing of mandatory meetings for each level of employee.
   • Outline a meeting agenda—a listing of basic topics to consider covering at every meeting including the last topic: Who else must know what was discussed and decided—supervisor, manager, executive, communications manager, editor, other?
   • Identify/provide supporting budget, equipment, facilities and material at every site.
   • Document the above and include in the plan.

3. Coordinate/Implement
  • Coordinate planned communications among management, supervision and employees.
  • Implement planned media and other tasks on a hourly/daily basis as defined in the communications manager's mission statement .

4.Monitor
  • Track progress weekly, if not daily.
  • Tap into the grapevine with embedded reporters to identify emerging issues, then address them on a weekly basis.
  • Review progress monthly with top managers to keep them engaged.
  • Measure goal attainment.
  • Audit the process for effectiveness annually. Poll employees on issues as needed.
  • Fine tune to intensify focus and fortify sustainment of achievement regularly.

Some may question the veracity and efficacy of what I have shared in this text. If so, they may just be missing the point. And that reminds me of a story, by Steve Derivan, I came across in the *Readers Digest*.

"Lou sees a sign in front of a house: "Talking Dog for Sale." Intrigued, he rings the bell and the owner shows him the dog.

"What's your story?" Lou asks.

The dog says, "I discovered I had this gift when I was a pup. The CIA signed me up, and soon I was jetting around the world, sitting at the feet of spies and world leaders, gathering important information and sending it back home. When I tired of that lifestyle, I joined the FBI, where I helped catch drug lords and gunrunners. I was wounded in the line of duty, received some medals, and now a movie is being make of my life."

"How much do you want for the dog?" Lou asks the owner.

"Ten dollars," says the owner.

Lou is incredulous. "Why on earth would you sell that remarkable dog for so little?"

"Because he's such a liar. He didn't do any of that stuff."

Like the owner who did not believe what his pet said and ignored a dog that talks, the reader may question whether I did all the stuff mentioned in this book and dismiss a communication system that works—it really does focus

<u>and sustain</u> achievement. It may be used in a variety of applications from public relations, marketing communications, organizational development and public affairs, to lobbying, campaigning for office, and politics. And used in any organization.

Before closing, I want to share some correspondence I had with Peter Drucker, the father of modern management, which I think lends some credibility to my system. I had followed his writings on management for years. His emphasis on planning and the employee as a resource was what I focused on.

In June of 2004, I wrote a letter to him "respectfully requesting" his comment concerning an article about Synchronous Communications in the *PR Journal*. The publication described it as a classic method to share internal information. The story was concise and thorough enough to present an excellent overview of the system and I thought that it would not require a lot of his time.

He mailed back my letter with a handwritten note at the bottom that stated "Sorry, this is well beyond my ken."

I wrote another letter in September of 2004 thanking him for his response and inquiring about any advice he could give me regarding publication of my book.

He again returned my letter with a note written at the bottom "Sorry, I am totally retired and don't see and/or advise anyone."

After release of *The Daily Drucker* in 2005, I thought that perhaps he had been too tied-up with that books' publication to find time for my request. I decided to give it one more try.

To dig deeper into his views on communications, I bought *The Essential Drucker* and *The Effective Executive* and found that:

- His statement that "communications are by and large just as poor today as they were twenty or thirty years ago" coincides with my experience. GM started internal communications in 1975 shortly after I was promoted into public relations. It has been a fragmented process across all organizations—until now with Synchronous Communications Management.
- He stated "downward communication has been the focus of management, whereas upward communication from subordinate to superior makes communications possible." SCM helps to coordinate and measure the flow of relevant information downward and upward. When SCM indicators for both downward and upward are high, it can be said that employees feel trusted and empowered because of dialogue.

- His view that "the focus on contribution leads to communications side-ways and thereby makes teamwork possible" is a unique element in SCM, of which few if any practitioners of communications are aware. I refer to it as lateral communications which is also measured by SCM. If down-ward, upward and lateral communications indicators are high, it can be said that employees will work autonomously, individually and collec-tively, to achieve organizational goals. All together, I define them as three-way communications—to, from and among employees. So, if employees feel empowered, they will communicate and work with fellow employees and management at any level because they know their role, they know what must be done and they feel trusted and empowered to do whatever has to be done. This is when achievement of organizational goals occurs—I call it Empowered Autonomy.
- The four fundamentals of communication he identified are right on the mark. Regarding the fourth one—"communication and information being different yet interdependent"—I use the term information-sharing. His term "shared experiences" captures the relationship in the same way.
- He suggested that communications involves communion. I had coined a term comm**union**cation to get managers to understand it is dialogue. That it is at least two-way, if not three way. Too many managers think that be-cause the organization has a newsletter it is communicating.

I was amazed by the similarities of our thinking on communications and wrote him another letter in July of 2005 with the above comparisons. I thought that maybe he would see that he does have the "ken."

I kept looking for his response to that letter. It never came.

I read in the newspaper a few months later that Peter Drucker died Novem-ber 11 at age 95.

I feel fortunate to have been personally "touched" and influenced by the fa-ther of public relations and the father of modern management. Hopefully, that influence will be recognized as Synchronous Communications Management.

In conclusion, for institutions of higher learning, I strongly recommend that serious consideration be given to Synchronous Communications Management's inclusion in courses such as management, marketing, organizational develop-ment, behavior and dynamics and even personnel and public relations. Perhaps going as far as to create a major curriculum would be a viable option. In doing so, it would open the field to more study, refinement and sophistication.

Although the urgency to do so may not be great, the positive impact of the deed could be of such magnitude that it would not only propel communications management to new levels of legitimacy and professionalism, it would immediately provide the necessary knowledge to boost management's effectiveness and organizational productivity to extraordinary heights.

Without top manager's awareness that communication is the only common thread that runs through every fabric of the organization, understanding that communication is the glue that holds the organization together, acceptance of the fact that communication is the only way to reach the hearts, minds and spirits of the people, and actionable support of communication as the organizations' most powerful strategic tool, change for the better will be slow and sporadic.

Think what could be accomplished if just 25 percent more employees get on board of their organizations bandwagon. Productivity would skyrocket, prices would decrease, the economy would improve domestically and globally, student achievement would rise, municipalities would provide more for the tax dollar, and community organizations would serve their constituencies more effectively. All of this and more because employees feel empowered with relevant information, understand the goals and their role, and are willing to work collaboratively with others for achievement.

Whatever the reluctance of organization's to robustly elevate the communication function and embrace the principles of the Synchronous Communications Management system, it must be overcome. Without that happening, the unit will be unable to sustain continuous improvement year-in and year-out, remain, unnecessarily, below its optimum level of performance and languish in the haze of its management's last frontier.

9

THE ADDENDUM

Explaining how strategic plan, culture management and Synchronous Communications Management fit together.

The total package of the three Actis Consulting change management systems depicted in the Actis Strategic Pyramid—Applied Management Effectiveness, Applied Culture Management and Synchronous Communications Management—helps to create focused, measured, and sustained human achievement.

Following descriptions of the Pyramid, there are illustrations of subcomponents of the systems: Model of Transition, Synchronous Communications Formula Model, Synchronous Communications Worksheet, Message Complexity vs Channel Selection Graph, Three-Way Communications Flow Chart, Employee Commitment/ Performance Model (Saginaw quality culture model) and the Achievement Culture Index.

ACTIS STRATEGIC PYRAMID

1. **Applied Management Effectiveness** provides the structure for the strategic plan which sets the focus for the organization and helps track progress using the Visible Strategies storyboard format. The plan is about what every discussion and decision in the organization should be based. Emerging issues should be identified, discussed, and by conscious decision, placed in the plan.

- **Vision**—ideal state of the organization three years hence. (An organization recognized for... A company that is...)
- **Missions**—role of top management to attain the vision, tactical role of every other employee level to attain the vision.
- **Critical Success Factors**—functions which must be performed effectively and efficiently to achieve the vision.
- **Action Strategies**—<u>what</u> steps must be taken to address each Critical Success Factor (starting the description of each step with a verb to denote action). The tactical mission and the <u>how-to</u> actions need to be decided at the tactical levels.
- **Visible Strategies**—documents and helps continuously track the status of Vision, Mission, Critical Success Factors and Action Strategies; every

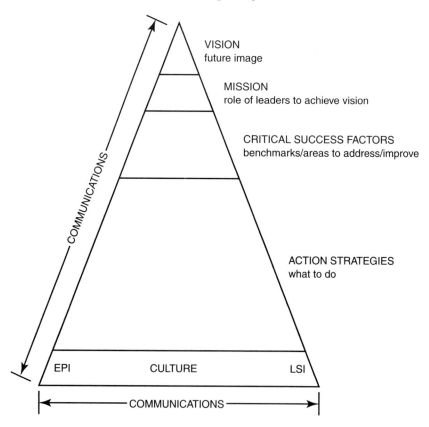

Actis Strategic Pyramid

VISION
future image

MISSION
role of leaders to achieve vision

CRITICAL SUCCESS FACTORS
benchmarks/areas to address/improve

ACTION STRATEGIES
what to do

COMMUNICATIONS

EPI   CULTURE   LSI

COMMUNICATIONS

issue is documented, dealt with and traced to completion; new issues are captured until adopted or discarded; motivates achievement of desired outcomes on time; provides snap-shot of planned progress and implementation.

2. **Applied Culture Management** identifies and measures management and employee behaviors, norms and values and represents the foundation of the pyramid - the human resources who translate the plan into action.
   - **Leadership Style Indicators (LSI)**—specific management behaviors of achievement, self-actualizing, encouraging, receptiveness.
   - **Employee Perception Indicators(EPI)**—employee perceptions of how they are expected to behave regarding achievement, self-actualizing, encouraging, receptiveness.

3. **Synchronous Communications Management** provides the framework to plan, organize, direct, control and communicate the flow of relevant information downward, upward, and laterally to the right audience at the right time by the right channels in order to focus and sustain a culture of achievement.

The "management" part of SCM follows:

Plan
- Define the vision—the ideal state of communications three years hence.
- Determine details of the 11-point SCM Worksheet to get the right information to the right audience at the right time through the right channels for each issue pertinent to the units strategic direction.
- Document everything that is to be done.

Organize
- Organize human, financial and physical resources.
- Decide the mission of the communications managers—their role in attaining the communication vision.
- Determine the communications philosophy—the role and tone of management, supervision and employees in the communications process.
- Establish an imbedded reporter network as a news source and as a grapevine and emerging issue monitor.
- Develop a meetings calendar—a listing of mandatory meetings for each level of employee.

- Outline a meeting agenda—a listing of basic topics to consider discussing at every meeting including the last topic: **Who else must know** what was discussed and decided—supervisor, manager, executive, communications department, editor, customer, supplier, other?
- Identify/provide supporting budget, equipment, facilities and material at every site.
- Document the above and include in the communication plan.

Coordinate/Implement
- Communicators must coordinate planned communications among management, supervision and employees.
- Communicators must implement planned media and other tasks on a hourly/daily basis as defined in the communications manager's mission statement and communications plan.

Monitor
- Track progress weekly, if not daily.
- Identify emerging issues, then address them on a weekly basis to decide relevancy to share them with the organization.
- Review progress monthly with top management to keep them engaged.
- Audit goal attainment per timetable; audit process annually.
- Fine tune, regularly, to intensify focus and fortify sustainment of achievement.

Subcomponents of the three systems follow:

Model of Transition—to make the transition from current beliefs and behaviors to the desired beliefs and behaviors, the organization and its management must consider what message is relevant and what actions are in line with that information. The two have to be in sync. Word and deed, and walk the talk must mesh.

Model of Transition from Current to Desired

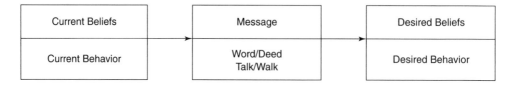

Current Beliefs	Message	Desired Beliefs
Current Behavior	Word/Deed Talk/Walk	Desired Behavior

Synchronous Communications Formula Model—to make the transition-from current beliefs/behaviors to desired beliefs/behaviors, relevant information flow must be managed to get the right message to the right audience at the right time through the right mix of channels (print, face-to-face, audio/video, symbolic). Research current beliefs and behaviors and obtain feedback from the audience to measure degree of beliefs and behavior change.

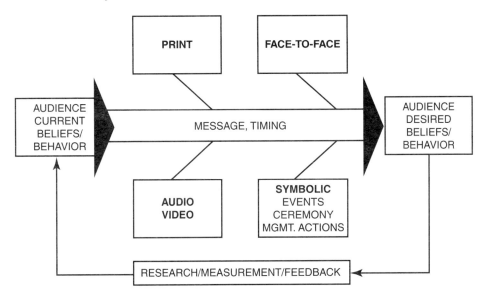

Synchronous Communications Formula Model

Synchronous Communications Formula
- Define Communications Issue
- Identify Specific Audiences for Issue
- Research Each Audiences Current Beliefs/Perceptions Concerning Issue
- Decide Desired Outcomes For Each Audience
- Identify/Develop Information/Messages
- Consider Print Channel
- Consider Face-to-Face Channel
- Consider Video/Audio Channel
- Consider Symbolic Channel
- Set Timing/Frequency of Message
- Establish Measurements of Success

Synchronous Communications Worksheet—a grid which serves as a tool and template for determining the content of the 11 elements of the Formula in sequence.

SYNCHRONOUS COMMUNICATIONS WORKSHEET

COMMUNICATIONS ISSUE:	
AUDIENCE	
CURRENT BELIEFS INTERESTS, PERCEPTIONS	
DESIRED BELIEFS, BEHAVIOR	
MESSAGES	
CHANNELS PRINT FACE-TO-FACE AUDIO, VIDEO SYMBOLIC	
TIMING FREQUENCY	
GOALS MEASUREMENTS (Quantify)	

<u>Message Complexity vs Channel Selection</u>—a graph which illustrates that the more complex the message or information the greater the need for face-to-face dialogue. One-on-one is the ultimate channel for sharing information.

Message Complexity vs Channel Selection Graph

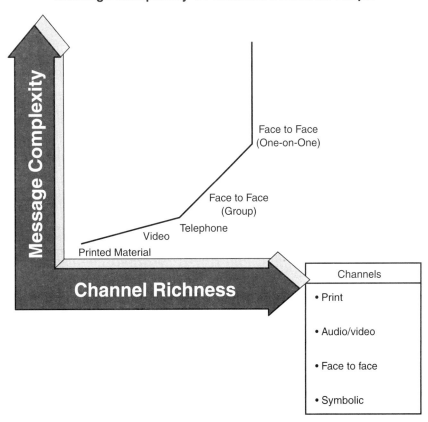

Three-Way Communications Flow Graph—if downward and upward information flow indicators are high (Employee Empowerment Indicators), employees feel empowered. If lateral information flow indicators are high (Employee Autonomy Indicators), employees feel empowered by information and are working autonomously with fellow employees.

Three-Way Communications Flow Graph

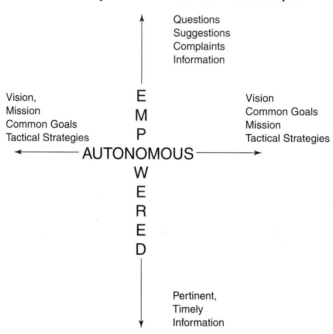

<u>**Employee Commitment/Performance Model**</u>—the Saginaw quality culture process model takes into account social values, the economic climate and job-related expectations and evaluates and compares them with the organizations' values. If employee perceptions show that the gap between needs and delivery is small, high commitment and strong supportive behavior in the form of discretionary effort result. If the gap is large, supportive behavior is weak.

Employee Commitment / Performance Model

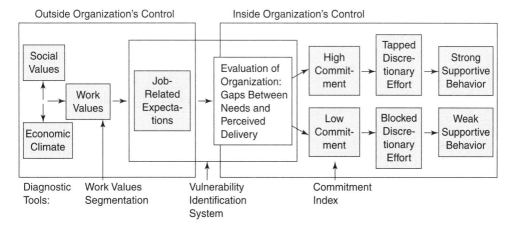

Leadership Style Indicators represent the identification and rating of specific behaviors that leaders exhibit in their every day decisions, communications and actions. This behavioral style sets the example for the rest of the organization and, formally or informally, defines how management expects the organization to perform, individually and collectively. The specific behaviors listed in the indicator may be ranked by the leaders themselves, to make them aware of how they "see" themselves, and/or rated by subordinates to compare with the self ranking. The 12-point circular profile chart, which follows, illustrates a constructive pattern of LSI.

Employee Perception Indicators are ranked by employees as the way they are expected to behave on the job. Employees rate these specific behavior's, on a scale of 1-5, to indicate whether they are expected to behave in that manner "not at all," "to a very great extent," or three choices in between. The 12-point circular profile chart, which follows, illustrates a constructive pattern of EPI.

Leadership Style Indicators Profile and Employee Perceptions Indicators Profile

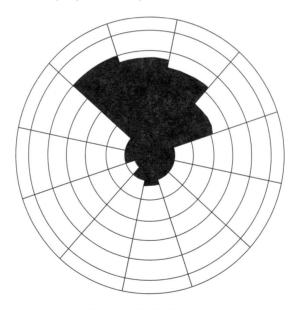

The chart reflects a constructive Leadership Style Indicator or constructive Employee Perceptions Indicator. Both sets of indicators are plotted on the same 12-point grid. Only the numerical graduations on the grid differ for each indicator.

<u>Achievement Culture Index</u>—a composite measurement of Leadership Style Indicators (specific, constructive behavioral norms), Employee Perception Indicators (employee perceptions of specific, management expectations of their behavior), Employee Empowerment Indicators (employee perceptions of downward and upward communications which measure empowerment) and Employee Autonomy Indicators (employee perceptions of lateral communications which measure autonomy). The maximum score is 100.

Taken altogether, the index tells us this:

- The degree to which management sets the right example, by word and deed, for achievement, self-actualizing, encouragement and receptiveness. (LSI)
- The degree to which employees perceive that example is expected of them. (EPI)
- The degree to which employees feel empowered by relevant information to follow that example. (EEI)
- The degree to which employees are working autonomously, individually and collectively, to achieve organizational goals. (EAI)

EDITORIAL CARTOONS

Relevant humor